EVERYTHING
YOU'VE HEARD IS
WRONG

[signature]

Phil 3:13-14

Also by Tony Campolo

> *Partly Right*
> *A Reasonable Faith*
> *It's Friday, But Sunday's Comin'*
> *You Can Make a Difference*
> *Who Switched the Price Tags?*
> *20 Hot Potatoes Christians Are Afraid to Touch*
> *The Kingdom of God Is a Party*
> *How to Be Pentecostal Without Speaking in*
>   *Tongues*

with Bart Campolo
> *Things We Wish We Had Said*

EVERYTHING YOU'VE HEARD IS WRONG

TONY CAMPOLO

WORD PUBLISHING
Dallas·London·Vancouver·Melbourne

Library of Congress Cataloging-in-Publication Data:

Campolo, Anthony.
    Everything you've heard is wrong / Anthony Campolo.
      p. cm.
   ISBN 0–8499–0934–1
   1. Success in business. 2. Business—Religious aspects—Christianity. 3. Business ethics. 4. Christian ethics. I. Title.
HF5386.C244 1992
174'.9658—dc20   92–26271
                                      CIP

Printed in the United States of America

2 3 4 5 9 LB 9 8 7 6 5 4 3 2 1

To Tom Roop

the founder of Bible Buzzards
a ministry that touched my life

Contents

Preface

Over the past decade I have been privileged to be a motivational speaker and a consultant for more than three hundred businesses and industries. The life insurance industry has been particularly receptive to me, and I have had the opportunity to share my ideas and beliefs with most of its major companies. As I have articulated the way in which biblical values and principles can be expressed in the marketplace, I have often been encouraged by my listeners to put my messages into writing. That is what led me to write this book.

Acknowledgments

I am a very dependent person, and I could not have put this book together without some very special people. Sue Dahlstrom, a close friend, and Debra Davidson, my niece, did the typing. Sue's husband, Tom, also my good friend, proofread and chauffeured the manuscript back and forth. And most important was my wife, Peggy, who did the editing. If these people had not been loving and patient, I would not have been able to get through the long and arduous process between writing and having a finished manuscript for my publisher. Here and now, I publicly say a heartfelt thank you to all of them. And if you enjoy and are helped by this book, you owe these people your thanks too.

Part 1

Love and Work

1

Everything You've Heard Is Wrong

I HAD SPENT THE AFTERNOON AT A sales conference sponsored by a large insurance corporation. The executives of the company had brought in an array of top-flight speakers to teach the sales force the most successful techniques for marketing their product. The audience listened with riveted attention as they were instructed how to "set up" clients, push the right emotional buttons, and close the deal. What they heard were the best insights about marketing that the experts in the field of behavioral psychology could provide. "Surefire" sales pitches were demonstrated that, according to the speakers, were certain to elicit the desired responses from even the most reluctant prospects. The presentations were brilliant!

It was my task to end the day with a motivational talk that could "psych up" the sales teams to get the job done. I was supposed to get the audience's juices flowing so that they would be enthused about doing the things they had been taught all day long. You can imagine the surprise, if not the shock, that greeted my opening words: "Everything you've heard today is wrong."

Disbelief ran across the faces of the company's executives. The director of the sales conference seemed to freeze in his crouched position by the sound control panel directly in front of the stage. And, as I surveyed the faces of the crowd, I knew I had their attention.

"People are not *things* to be manipulated with the right techniques," I said. "They are not Pavlovian dogs. We do not have a right to set them up to respond to the 'proper' stimuli in order to elicit the 'proper' response. They are not creatures to be *used* to further our own economic self-interest. People are sacred! Each of them is an infinitely precious person in whom the Eternal God has chosen to make His home. And all of them deserve to be treated with reverent respect.

"Too often, in our attempt to get people to buy what we're selling, we approach them as though they were less than human. Too frequently, we relate to them as though they were objects instead of subjects. Too easily, we learn to have with them what the great Jewish philosopher, Martin Buber, called 'I-It' relationships rather than 'I-Thou' relationships. People whom we encounter in the marketplace deserve better. They are entitled to a measure of awe and wonder and even a bit of love."

I sensed that the audience was coming along with me. It was as though they were relieved to learn that the uneasiness they had experienced about the manipulative techniques being taught to them had been justified. There were even heads nodding in agreement with what had at first seemed like some off-the-wall statements. The whole sales conference was taking on a new tone and even the executives of the company seemed to welcome it.

"You don't have to manipulate people if you're selling something they really need," I explained. "All you have to do is show them the seriousness of their need and then demonstrate how what you have to offer can meet that need.

"You're selling life insurance!" I declared. "That's something people really *do* need for the security of their families. Recognize that! And if you're selling something that people really need, then why do you lower yourself to play these manipulative sales tricks? You only end up degrading your clients if you treat them as unsuspecting targets of a sales pitch. And you lower yourself if you take a noble profession like selling insurance that people need and turn it into the work of a con artist."

16

Then I went on to tell them this remarkable story. Some years ago, Martin England, a white, Southern insurance salesman, learned that the great Martin Luther King, Jr. was not covered with an adequate life insurance policy. He worried about that almost daily. This insurance agent became so concerned that he began to try to contact Dr. King to sell him the kind of family protection plan that would insure the future well-being of King's family should anything happen to him. It wasn't easy getting to Martin Luther King. This determined salesman followed King for weeks, trying to tell the civil rights leader that he had a gigantic and urgent need. Finally he got his opportunity. He sat Martin Luther King down, explained his need for life insurance, and got the necessary papers signed.

It was not long afterward that an assassin's bullet pierced King's body and took from America the greatest of all the modern spokespersons for freedom. Fortunately, the tragedy of King's death was not compounded by his leaving behind a destitute family. An ordinary insurance man had taken care of matters through an extraordinary commitment to meet a very important need.

When I finished, the crowd was on its feet cheering, and the president of the company was leading the applause. He wanted his sales staff to be more than money grubbers. He wanted them to be proud of themselves and what they did to make a living.

That is what this book is about. It is designed to help those who believe that there is an alternative to the view of the marketplace as a jungle. It is meant to inspire those who want to make personal relationships in the business world into real friendships. And it is a book that I hope will provide some suggestions as to how to make "love" a verb both in the office and on the assembly line.

In this book, there will be no apology for talking about God and His love. This is because I know what can happen when the affairs of a business and the relationships of people in the workaday world are guided by the hand of God instead of the invisible hand of iron-fisted economics which makes profits the bottom line of all.

There will be no excuses made for appeals to the heart, because the message here is about caring in a realm of life that too often has been characterized by indifference and coldness.

But most of all, this is a book about a way of doing business that works. It is a refutation of the cynics who claim that the values and principles laid down in the Bible mitigate against success in the dog-eat-dog world of commerce and industry. It is as strong a declaration as I can make that, in a world where everything seems to be measured by dollar signs, we can do well by doing good.

If you are thinking that this book sounds more like a philosophy book than like a typical book on management, you're right! The trouble with most books on management is that they are too focused on the mechanics of increasing efficiency and pay little or no attention to more basic questions.

Management experts usually answer the question of *how* to get things done more efficiently without asking *why* we are doing what we are doing. They show what particular organizational techniques will accomplish without exposing what will happen to the people involved in the process.

Those in marketing usually spell out how to motivate a sales staff and sharpen the sales pitch so as to improve the bottom line. But they often do this without asking whether there is a bottom line to life itself that is being ignored or violated.

In college business courses or in typical MBA programs, there is almost no attention given to such philosophical questions as: Who am I? What is my mission in life? Does my job provide a viable means to live out that mission?

It is often presumed that philosophy is for eggheads and that business people should be concerned about more practical things. Philosophical questions may be intriguing, but after all, they do not help us make more money.

Too often there is a prideful disdain for "ultimate questions" on the part of those who are caught up in the everyday round of making and selling things. People who do ask philosophical questions are viewed by hard-nosed business types as being detached from *real* life, or having their heads in the clouds. Those who have embraced the so-called practical world of business at times consider those who probe the *meanings* of things as being caught up in abstractions that lead nowhere.

"Pragmatism! That's the only philosophy that really matters," they say. "We want to know what works! What brings results! What's been *proven* to be successful in everyday life."

I contend that there is nothing *more* practical than asking ultimate questions. I say that there is nothing *more* important than exploring the whys and the wherefores of life. In the end, I argue, if the ultimate questions about who we are, what we are doing, and what it all means are not answered, then everything will come to nothing in the end.

As I look at what is going on in the business world and consider what is happening to those who live out their lives in the marketplace, I realize that asking and answering ultimate questions may be the most pragmatic of all activities. After careful observation, I confidently conclude that coming up with answers to some of the basic philosophical questions about what we are doing with our lives may be the most practical of all possible ventures.

This book will not allow you to escape philosophical questions, especially as they relate to your life in the world of business and industry. As one who would be your friend, I cannot allow you to go about what is sometimes called "the mundane activity of making a living" without facing up to at least three questions. These questions must be answered if you are to live any kind of successful life. They are:

1. If I'm going to be a person I can live with: *What kind of person am I going to be?*
2. If I'm going to do something meaningful with my life: *What kind of work should I do?*
3. And as my life comes to an end: *What do I want my legacy to be?*

Answering these questions becomes one of life's forced options. You must have answers. And if I were in your place, I wouldn't leave home without them.

2

The Basic Questions

GOOD BUSINESS REQUIRES THAT YOU know *what* you are doing. But even more importantly, it requires that you know *why* you are doing it. This latter concern is what eventually will force you to deal with the basic inquiries that must be made about your life.

The first question has to do with character. It has to do with the qualities that you want to be evident in your personality. This question may be the most important question of all. Upon reflection, you will probably agree that the kind of person you are will, to a great extent, determine the kind of work that you do.

Your "doing," if you stop to think about it, flows from your "being." As a case in point, what Mother Teresa *does* is an inevitable consequence of the kind of person she *is*. She works with the poor and suffering people of Calcutta *because* she *is* a loving and kind person.

Some years ago when my son Bart was in the third grade, he was given the assignment of preparing a talk with the title, "What I Am Going to Be When I Grow Up."

Facetiously, I told him that the teacher had asked him the wrong question, and that what she really wanted to know was what he was going to *do* to make money when he grew up. I even suggested that he say to the teacher, "What I am going to *be* is a fully actualized human being like Jesus, and I haven't yet made up my mind what I'm going to do to make money."

Fortunately, my son did not heed my advice. I doubt if my suggestion would have gone over very well.

But the point is that there *is* a difference between what you *are* and what you *do.* The former has to do with character while the latter has to do with action.

Most people realize that they are responsible for their actions. They recognize that what they *do* in their everyday lives is the result of countless decisions that they are making daily. However, there are many people who do not realize that their character or lack of it is also something that is chosen. Character is not so much a given as it is the result of decisions.

Every day, you make many, many decisions that determine who you *are.* In reality, hour by hour you must not only decide what you are going to do on any given day; you must also decide what kind of person you are going to *be.* You do not decide once. You decide over and over again in each and every situation and circumstance in life. And the cumulative result of all that decision making establishes your identity. Through the process of deciding how you will react to the people and circumstances that confront you constantly, you establish who and what you are. You become a particular kind of person, and you establish a more and more definitive character. Over time, people will come to know who and what you are. And what is more important, *you* will come to know who you are. The decisions that determine your character are in your own hands.

More often than I care to admit, I meet people who do not grasp the truth that it is they themselves who decide who and what they are. They seem to think that genes, DNA, or social conditions determine the kinds of persons we become. It is common to find people who, when asked why they are the way they are, shrug their shoulders and say something like, "I suppose I was born this way," or "It's the way I was brought up."

Certainly, the courses we take in college entitled "Behaviorism" or "Socio-biology" do not help us to take responsibility for who we are. There are all kinds of "scientific" findings that can lend support to the claim that a person's character is not chosen but instead is *determined* by sociological and social forces beyond his or her control. But while I will readily admit that inherited traits strongly influence each and every one of us, and while I also agree that social conditioning impacts everyone's personality, I must strongly affirm that ultimately everyone can and does choose the kind of person he or she wills to be. With intense conviction I contend that each of us is given by God the freedom that can enable us to rise above those powerful influences on character and become totally other than any scientist could have predicted. All of us have seen those individuals who, in terms of lineage and upbringing, should be shiftless, uncaring adults but through the exercising of their own decision-making power have become good and loving persons.

It is the thesis of this book that every person is responsible for what he or she becomes. Your being—or shall I say your character—is yours to create through the decisions you make. If your character is flawed, you do not have the right to say that's just the way I am.

What Kind of Work Should I Do?

As suggested above, what we *do* for a living should be an inevitable consequence of who we are. What we determine to be should strongly influence what each of us decides to do to earn a living. Furthermore, we are only kidding ourselves if we think we can earn a living in a way that contradicts the kind of person we want to be.

A friend of mine, a well-known teenage television actress, was asked to play a role in which she would portray a high school girl who gets pregnant and then gets out of her predicament by having an abortion. I was really pleased when she told me that she had turned down the part, even though her decision so angered her agent and the show's producer that it may prove to cost her dearly in terms of her hopes for a successful career. I was even more pleased when she told me her reasons. "It wasn't just the bad influence that I would have on others that convinced me it was the wrong thing to do," she explained. "It was what the part would do to me. I do not think I could have played that role for very long without being changed inside."

Of course she was right. What we do does strongly influence who and what we are, even as who and what we are strongly influences what we do. Many people do not realize that actors and actresses are not the only ones who play roles. All of us, as Shakespeare once suggested, are players on a stage. And the roles that we play out, whether in the office or the factory, impact our character. It is difficult, if not impossible, to sustain a role at work that is out of character. Sooner or later, who we are will be influenced by the role we play at work. In the terminology of the theater, it is best if we choose roles that are typecast for us. It is crucial that what we choose to do in life to earn a living be in harmony with the character traits we wish to possess. Too many people do not recognize that and find themselves unable to escape the transforming influences of what they have chosen to do.

What Do I Want My Legacy to Be?

This third question is seldom deemed important by young people. I often hear them say things like, "What do I care what people say about me when I'm dead? Once I'm gone it really doesn't make any difference."

Note that I said *young* people. This is not the sort of thing that I ever hear from older people. As I close in on sixty years of age, I become increasingly aware of my encroaching mortality. As death rushes toward me, I care more and more about how I will be remembered. I am gaining insight into my mother's thinking when, knowing that death was near, she meticulously planned her own funeral in a way that would make plain those things that really mattered to her. And my mother talked to me in detail about how she wanted to be remembered.

On the tombstone of one famous English poet are inscribed the words, "I have plowed the water." In a very similar vein, a cynical Greek philosopher trying to illustrate his belief that once we are dead we leave no trace of our existence, put his thumb in a pail of water. Then upon removing it, he asked his students, "Where is the hole that my finger once made?" The famous poem, "Leaves of Grass," by Walt Whitman picks up the

26

same theme concerning the transitory nature of our accomplishments. In the poem, Whitman reminds us that all the victories and defeats on the great battlefields of the world are, in the end, conquered and covered by grass.

In the face of such nihilism, there are those of us who are people of faith and believe that what we do *can* make a difference. In the words of the apostle Paul, while much of what is done in this life is meaningless and will be burned away, it is possible to choose to do things that will have lasting significance long after we are gone.

> According to the grace of God which is given unto me, as a wise masterbuilder, I have laid the foundation, and another buildeth thereon. But let every man take heed how he buildeth thereupon. For other foundation can no man lay than that is laid, which is Jesus Christ. Now if any man build upon this foundation gold, silver, precious stones, wood, hay, stubble; Every man's work shall be made manifest: for the day shall declare it, because it shall be revealed by fire; and the fire shall try every man's work of what sort it is. If any man's work abide which he hath built thereupon, he shall receive a reward. If any man's work shall be burned, he shall suffer loss: but he himself shall be saved; yet so as by fire.
>
> 1 Corinthians 3:10–15

Each of us, when leaving this earth, will crave to know that we have left behind something of significance. And each of us hopes that his or her legacy is good and will be honored as such. There are philanthropists who give with the hope that buildings on university campuses will be named after them. There are authors who fantasize about writing books that will stand the test of time and become classics. There are soldiers who bravely go to their deaths dreaming of ballads being written about them and sung to future generations. The idea that, when our lives are ended, nothing significant will remain is not only intolerable, but, I contend, it is also untrue.

Because of the universal craving for some kind of legacy that will give significance to our living, each of us wants to achieve something in life that will live on after we are gone.

Each of us wants to accomplish something of worth, to live out some glorious mission. And that is ultimately what our vocational life should be all about.

The right job should be a calling. The best vocation should be the living out of a dream or a vision of doing something great for others. "Where there is no vision, the people perish" (Prov. 29:18).

And so the questions must be asked. What kind of person do you want to be? What kind of work will be worthy of your humanity? And when you die, how do you want to be remembered? These questions cannot be avoided. Even if you repress them by day, they will haunt you by night.

When these questions are properly answered, your work and your relationships at work will be meaningful. These questions will stimulate energetic labor and will propel you toward great accomplishments. These questions must be answered so that you will know whether or not you are a successful human being.

There's an old joke about an airliner out over the ocean. The pilot announces, "Well folks, we have some bad news and some good news. The bad news is that we're lost! The good news is that we're making record time!"

Those who do not ask and answer the ultimate questions about life may be making record time so far as career advancement is concerned. But if they do not know where they are going in life, their record-making advancements will prove to be absurd and ludicrous in the end.

Socrates was right, and every person in every vocation should hear his words, "The unexamined life is not worth living."

3

Who Do You Think You Are, Anyway?

FOLLOWING WORLD WAR II THERE WERE more than two hundred Frenchmen who returned to Paris suffering from amnesia. They had been in Japanese prison camps and had suffered through a horrible ordeal of privation and torture. These men had been so psychologically devastated by their imprisonment that they had lost the conscious awareness of who they were and from where they had come.

In most cases, their identities were quickly established from Red Cross records or with the help of fellow prisoners. But there were thirty-two men whose identities seemed impossible to ascertain. There seemed to be no records of them nor anyone who knew anything about them. The doctors who were treating these thirty-two men believed that their chances for recovery would be slim if not impossible, unless they were connected with former friends and relatives and restored to their once-familiar settings.

Someone proposed publishing photographs of the men on the front page of newspapers throughout the country and giving a date and time when anyone having information about any of these amnesia victims should come to the Paris Opera House. The plan worked! On the proper day and at the assigned time, a crowd gathered to view these sad war veterans. In dramatic fashion, the first of the amnesia victims walked onto the stage of the darkened opera house, stood in the spotlight, and slowly turned completely around. Before the hushed audience, he pleadingly and softly inquired, "Does anybody out there know who I am?"

These men were lucky. They had the chance to ask the question out loud. For most of us the question is muted. We would like to ask it, but we are ashamed. We don't want to blow the cover of self-assuredness and self-confidence behind which we cower in fear. So the question remains buried and our self-doubt concealed. But there are many of us who, in spite of our pretenses, are not sure who we are and what our lives are all about. In many more cases than might be surmised, there are those of us who are not sure that we should be doing what we're doing nor are we convinced that our lives are being lived out with any real significant purpose. Everywhere I go I meet people who are ready to make a major life change because of discontent with what they are but do not do so because they haven't the slightest idea of what they should become. If people do not know who they are, they have a hard time figuring out what they're supposed to be doing with their lives.

Sociologists contend that the problem of determining a clear identity is a Herculean task, because life in the modern urban setting not only allows, but encourages us to establish multiple identities. In my own case, if I spend the early morning with my immediate family, at breakfast they provide for me the identity of "Dad." I'm not only the family "breadwinner," but I play out the role of an "imp of fun" that destroys the formalities associated with the Victorian patriarch and makes me into my children's "big buddy."

But when I leave my family and go downtown to deliver a special lecture at the university, I leave the identity of "Dad" behind me. In the halls of academia, I take on the identity of DOCTOR CAMPOLO, "that specialist who attempts to define personal existential existence in the context of the contemporary *Weltanschauung.*"

In the afternoon, I travel out to Eastern College and take up the identity provided by informal relationships which I have with fellow Christians who are my students and friends. There I become simply "Tony."

Then, in the evening, I go out to preach at some church, and the people there provide me with still another identity. To those in the congregation I become "Saint Anthony."

At the end of the day I am tempted to look in the mirror and ask the probing and difficult question, "Will the *real* Tony Campolo please step forward?" In the course of a day I have played out so many different roles for so many different groups, each of which provides its own definition of "self" for me, that I have great difficulty figuring out just who I really am. And when I am confronted by Jesus, who asks of me, as He did of the demoniac who met Him by the sea two thousand years ago, "Who are you? What's your name?" I, like many others, am apt to answer, "I am Legion, because I am many."

A common pitfall on the way to establishing identity is to allow ourselves to be defined by whatever job we happen to fall into when we finish school. Our being becomes our doing. Who we are is established by what we do. It's all so easy and natural that we hardly notice its happening. Without even realizing it, we can "slip-slide away" into letting the identities provided by our work become the "ultimate" basis for defining who we are.

Of course the problem with letting our jobs provide our identities is that sooner or later we all lose our jobs. Whether it comes sooner through layoffs or later through retirement, it will happen. And then, for those whose identities have been wrapped up primarily in their work, there is a horrendous crisis. Who of us has not encountered those persons who are devoid of any identity or meaning to their lives because all that they were was synonymous with their job? So many, particularly men, die very shortly after retirement simply because they cannot figure out any good reason for living.

Back in the 1950s, William Whyte, Jr. wrote a series of articles for *Fortune* magazine which were later incorporated into a book entitled *The Organization Man.* In a disturbing manner, Whyte probed the character (or lack thereof) of businessmen and women like the ones to be seen today waiting to fly away at most airports. He explored how the identities derived from their "professional positions" determined almost everything about them, from the kind of wives they *must* have (remember this book was written back in the '50s!) and the kind of children they are supposed to have, to the way in which they think, vote, and even pray. As you read Whyte's book you will be struck with the validity of his arguments. Most people in business, he claimed, allow the definition of self provided by their jobs to be the basis of who they are and how their lives will be lived.

In a more scholarly manner, David Reisman takes Whyte's argument one step further. With Reisman, the case is made that from early childhood on, Americans are socialized to play out roles that will gain them success regardless of what personal compromises must be made in terms of ethics and values. He argues that those who want to "make it" in our world must become "other-directed" persons who have little integrity of personhood and are more than willing to become what the people at work expect them to be.

A more modern sociologist, Irving Goffman, paints an even more troubling image of those of us who establish our identities by means of our jobs. Goffman refers to us as "con artists." In our jobs we do not so much learn the skills required to accomplish our assigned tasks, as we develop a way to act and "present ourselves," that will convince those around us that we are "professionals" who know what we're doing. In the end, according to Goffman, we are nothing but con artists who survive by fooling people into thinking that we are more than we really are, and who lack any core self that stands behind the many "conning" roles that we play out in the workplace.

In Arthur Miller's play, *Death of a Salesman,* the main character, Willy Loman, believes that the secret of success lies in "personality." The glad hand, the engaging personality, and the good "first appearance" all blend together to establish a person whom people really like.

The "cult of personality" as personified in the life of Willy Loman has become, in recent years, a bit passé. New models for success have crowded it out, and new techniques for "working with people" effectively have been devised.

We All Get Found Out

Once upon a time there was an office manager who lost his job during a recession. In his sadness he wandered into a park, found himself an empty bench, and sat down. After a while another man came strolling along. This second man was especially sad as he took a seat at the opposite end of the bench.

After these two men had sat silently for a couple of hours, the first man said, "I'm an office manager who has been made redundant. I don't have a job anymore. What's your problem?"

The second man answered, "I own a circus. The big attraction at my circus was an ape. Last week the ape died, and the crowds have fallen off to almost nothing. I think I'm going to be out of business if I don't find another ape."

It did not take long for the first man to come up with an interesting proposal. "You need an ape and I need a job. What if I dress up in the ape's skin and pretend to be real? I could carry on for your patrons and everybody would be happy."

Having nothing to lose, the circus owner decided to give it a try. To his surprise the fake ape proved to be more exciting and drew larger crowds than the real one had. Money came pouring in. And both the former office manager and the circus owner were getting rich.

Then, one day, things got out of hand. Somehow a lion got into the same cage with the fake ape. The office manager didn't know what to do. He maneuvered as best he could to escape the claws of the lion but realized that sooner or later he would be a goner.

A large crowd gathered outside the cage to watch the spectacle. They screamed and gasped as the lion finally trapped the office manager in a corner of the cage and poised himself to leap on the make-believe ape. Suddenly, the shocked crowd heard the ape yell in a shaken, frightened voice, "Help! Help!"

It was then that the lion muttered under his breath, "Shut up, stupid! Do you think you're the only one around here that's out of a job?"

Sooner or later we all get found out. Sooner or later we all blow our cover. It is only a matter of time before who and what we really are becomes obvious to everyone. Any attempt to conceal our true nature will eventually come to naught. In some stressful, off-guarded moment, who and what we are will surface. There is no point in pretending. Who we are and what we are, sooner or later, according to the Bible, "will be declared from the rooftops."

But there is an even more important reason for establishing a real identity than the fear of exposure. It is that when you establish a well-defined "inner" character you will be able to sleep better at night. You will be at peace with yourself. Being sure of who you are will enable you to be comfortable with yourself, and hence, be comfortable with everyone around you. When you have established personal integrity, you will radiate confidence in your interactions with others. And that confidence will serve you well in all you have to do. When the goodness you want to project outwardly is true of you inwardly, when what you appear to be is not just a skin you put on, you can live at peace with yourself and the rest of the world.

4

Some Have It— Some Don't

A FEW YEARS AGO, THE Howard Fischer Associates, one of New York's top executive search firms, conducted a survey of CEOs of the top one hundred companies in the New York area to find out what character traits are valued most by leaders. They were interested in what traits junior executives should cultivate in themselves in order to become the kinds of corporate leaders who would be deemed most desirable. While honesty and fairness ranked highest, there were other important character traits that were cited. The advice of these top CEOs went like this:

> Never compromise on matters of principle nor standards of excellence, even on minor issues.
>
> Be persistent and never give up.
>
> Have a vision of where you are going and communicate it often.
>
> Know what you stand for, set high standards, and don't be afraid to take on tough problems despite the risk.
>
> Spend less time managing and more time leading. Lead by example.

Bring out the best in others. Hire the best people you can find, then delegate authority and responsibility, but stay in touch.

Have confidence in yourself and in those around you, and trust others.

Accept blame for failures and credit others with success. Possess integrity and personal courage.

Certainly we do not find in this list compiled by those who have become corporate leaders anything of the "cutthroat" qualities that were so evident in the robber barons and tycoons of earlier decades. Indeed, it is a "gentler and kinder" leader who is sought. It seems as though the whole corporate world is looking for leaders with "character" who reflect traits and values that come from religious traditions.

Unfortunately, most business managers and salespeople who are seeking models are not paying much attention to these top executives. Instead, they have bought into the "clever" techniques of those "hot shots" who see the secrets of success in the insights of "pop" psychology. What is seen and heard at most management and sales conferences are shortcuts to success, even though they supposedly are based on the most advanced "scientific" discoveries of modern psychology and sociology.

Before I go any further to try to explain how to develop the traits of a good character, I think I should at least outline what is commonly being passed off these days as "sound" advice for achieving success. Before exploring the ways in which we might address the ultimate questions about what we should be doing with our lives and what we can accomplish that might have enduring significance, it would be useful to examine the "techniques" that so many motivational speakers at business conferences promote as the means to wealth, health, and happiness.

In an effort to become a supersuccessful entrepreneur, people embrace a variety of models. Some have sought to become more effective by trying to optimize their use of time. The successful person to them is the time-efficient person.

They are convinced that things like making lists that prioritize what needs to be done and designating the proper amount of time to tasks in accord with their importance will assure that their goals will be reached and their lives marked by great achievements.

Others have sought the secret of how to be a success in business in the "team player" model. It is built on the new "in" idea that "synergy" (a special kind of creative energy) emerges when colleagues test out ideas and concepts in "creative discussion." Those who believe that being a good team player is the way to become a top achiever work hard on developing the traits associated with teamwork.

Still others see the secret of success in the ability to motivate others. These people think that those who accomplish the most are the ones who can "turn on" others with their visions and dreams. They long to be able to speak with such convincing power that everyone around them will be energized. They believe that with proper communication skills they can get others to give themselves wholeheartedly to the work that needs to be done if success is to be realized.

These methods, along with many other models for effective sales and management, have their place. Each, in its own way, provides *some* good advice. Each, when analyzed, embodies certain vital truths. It is no wonder that the books that herald these ideas sell so well. However, all such models have their limitations, and when each has been tried and tested, I think we will find that something much more profound is needed. After all the new and innovative tricks have been put into practice, there is still a sense that what we have is not enough. All of these methods for achieving success have shortcomings. What ends do each of these good means serve? When properly utilized, what worthwhile purpose will be realized by employing them? Is what we have here some excellent means without any clearly defined and intrinsically valuable goals?

One day while living as a recluse in Maine, Henry David Thoreau noticed that his privacy was being invaded by a group of workmen. When he investigated these strangers, he discovered that they were putting up some wires that were part of a new-fangled invention called the telegraph.

"Haven't you heard?" asked one of the workmen. "They have invented the telegraph! And now the people in Florida can instantaneously communicate with the people in Maine!"

"How wonderful!" responded Thoreau. But then upon reflection, he asked, "But what if the people in Florida have nothing to say to the people in Maine?"

It should be obvious that clearly defined goals and purposes worthy of our humanity are essential if we are to be people who know what our lives in general and our work in particular are really all about. We must become a people who delve deeper and work harder to establish a sense of what our existence and our labor is meant to achieve. However, we tend to shy away from such arduous challenges because our culture has made us leery of theology and almost indifferent to philosophy. We will take almost any other path to provide us with meaning and guidance. We will become almost anything else, but we are not about to become philosophers or theologians.

Pop Psychology as an Answer

Ours is an age in which one of the primary sources for guidance in how to manage a business and how to be effective in sales is in psychology. This is not surprising since we have become a people steeped in respect for anything that sounds scientific. Our respect for science and our almost fanatical belief that there are scientific answers to most of our problems lead us to place our confidence in the directives of psychological research.

Because psychology gives the illusion of being empirically scientific, we tend to take what we learn from this discipline and employ it, without critiquing it, to answer most of life's questions. This is not to say that a great deal of what is touted by the "pop" psychologists who regularly turn up as guest speakers at sales and management conferences is not useful. But it should be realized that a significant amount of what is presented at those business conference "pep rallies" is "fluff" being paraded in the guise of "ultimate truth."

Perhaps the most common of all the messages being communicated by these popular "experts" in managerial psychology is an overblown emphasis on self-esteem. An underlying theme in most of these presentations is that people who feel good about themselves inevitably prove to be the most productive. What often comes across in this supposedly easiest of all shortcuts to effectiveness is the idea that if employees have a positive self-concept, then all else will follow.

There is some truth in all of this. But before we get carried away with this gospel of self-esteem, we should realize that some of the most effective workers in the world today are the Japanese. Personality tests will reveal that the Japanese people have very low self-images and are usually depressed because they do *not* feel good about themselves. I think self-esteem is essential for happiness, but it may not be as easily correlated with economic success as is sometimes assumed.

Americans everywhere have religiously believed in the good that can be derived from self-esteem. They have taken this idea and played it out to absurd limits. From the time our children are born, we shower them with constant affirmation of their worth and value. Most teenagers have rooms filled with trophies, medals, and plaques. They seem to get impressive recognition for even the slightest achievements. It seems as though we are so anxious to enhance the self-images of our youngsters that we give them prizes just for showing up.

There is no need to win a championship or do something noble; recognition of "greatness" is handed out to everyone regardless of accomplishment. In school, sloppy work is praised and lazy efforts are greeted with cheers from both teachers and parents. "We've got to build up our kids, no matter what," we keep telling ourselves.

We need to be careful about overdoing this self-esteem thing. There are many indications that the constant praising of youngsters for their work, regardless of the degree of effort they have made or the level of achievement attained, may actually be encouraging mediocrity. After all, if youngsters get accolades for doing little, what incentive is there for doing more? If laziness and half-hearted efforts are enthusiastically accepted, will it not follow that children will become satisfied with themselves even though they demonstrate a low level of achievement?

"Why exhaust yourself in hard work?" they might ask themselves. "What I am doing is more than good enough."

There are those who think that attempts to build self-esteem in the workplace will result in all kinds of successful payoffs. But while there can be numerous benefits derived from building up the self-esteem of workers, we also should realize that some sorry results can come from all of this. One Christian organization that I studied overdid it. They made a practice of constantly praising their workers, even when there was little that deserved praise. They kept telling them in exaggerated fashion that their sacrificial Christian service was deeply appreciated and that they were accomplishing more than anyone could have expected. The workers, who in reality were being paid quite well, according to going rates for office work, were hardly sacrificing. Yet they were made to feel that they were going the second mile for Jesus and that they deserved much more pay for their labors than they were receiving.

This attempt to provide positive affirmation ended up backfiring. The workers started to believe all of the flattering rhetoric and gradually came to feel perfectly justified in doing less than they could or should.

As the work output of these overpaid workers fell, they reminded their affirming employers that they were "sacrificing for Jesus" and that any criticism of their work was a poor way of showing gratitude "after all that they had done."

I know of one young man who actually quit because he was made to feel that in being so sacrificially Christian, he was allowing himself to be underpaid and exploited by his employers. He had a rude awakening when he discovered that the secular organization in which he later found a job paid him less and expected more. But this young man soon adjusted to reality. Without all the false flattery that he had previously known, he gained a realistic view of his value in the marketplace. When faced with the truth, he no longer felt exploited.

Self-esteem psychology can make many positive contributions, but let us be careful that we don't overdo it. The Bible teaches us to remember that we ought not think more highly of ourselves than we ought to think, but instead should think realistically (Rom. 12:3). The apostle Paul writes:

> For if a man think himself to be something, when he is nothing, he deceiveth himself. But let every man prove his own work, and then shall he have rejoicing in himself alone, and not in another. For every man shall bear his own burden.
>
> Galatians 6:3–5

Giving praise to people who have not borne their burdens or carried out their responsibilities is very wrong and can be damaging to all involved. But what is more important is that the good feelings that come from praise can never provide the kind of gratification and fulfillment that comes from being a person of goodness and integrity and from living a meaningful life.

The Human Potential Movement

Some of the "experts" who do speaking and consulting for today's business organizations see the answer to life and success in the human potential movement. They claim that employees should expect to be fulfilled human beings within the context of their jobs. "Actualizing one's individuality" in the workaday world is preached as a necessary payoff for daily labor. Workers are made to feel that it is an employer's responsibility to provide them with gratifying jobs.

Of course, work that is completely fulfilling is desirable, but unfortunately it is rare. Jobs that provide psychological ecstasy are generally not easily found. Even those jobs that seem to be the most glamorous carry with them a certain amount of grunt work. And even those jobs that seem to promise nonstop fulfilling excitement often include long stretches of boring mundane tasks to carry out.

As I looked at a recent ad inviting young people to join the army, I realized that the human potential movement had even help to mold what I view on television. The singing voices in the background of the ad called out to young viewers: "Be all that you can be!"

This wonderful invitation was sung against a backdrop of dramatic war games, paratroopers jumping out of planes, commandos scaling cliffs, jet pilots soaring into the sky, and young men visiting exotic foreign cities were all thrown up on the screen.

The army is not really what the ads tell us it is. Please don't get me wrong. Going into the army *may* be the best thing that a young person can do in preparation for later life. But the good that the army does for recruits is not accomplished by providing them with a constant stream of exciting and entertaining things to do. Quite the contrary! The army often does young people a lot of good precisely because it forces them to do what they might *not* want to do.

Most of life is not "going at it at your own pace" and always enjoying what you are doing. The real army does a good job of getting many young people used to this reality and hence makes them more fit to take their places in the real world.

In retrospect, for all the good that the human potential movement may have done in the typical workplace, there is some evidence that it also may have created some discontent and frustration. By nurturing in people unrealistic ideas of what they can get from their jobs, some have been rendered unhappy.

Too commonly the expectation generated by the gurus of the human potential movement is that ultimate gratification of the psyche can be gained through jobs and that jobs will allow us to actualize our personhood. Many an employer has had to endure the complaints of spiritually empty and emotionally restless workers who blame the workplace for their malaise. What these unhappy people really need is that sense of fulfillment that comes from being a person with character and possessing a clear sense of purpose and meaning for his or her life.

5

The Crux
of the Matter

ONE HOT SUMMER EVENING I WAS WALKING on the boardwalk at Ocean City, New Jersey. Confronting me head on was a little girl. At most she was six years old. She was carrying a tube of paper topped off with a fluffy pile of cotton candy, the pink stuff that is mostly air but takes up a lot of room. In this case, the cotton candy was a couple of feet high and about a foot wide.

I had to laugh when I saw the bright-eyed little girl and her oversized treat. "How can a little girl like you eat *all* of that candy?" I asked.

Without a moment's hesitation she answered me, "Well, you see mister, I'm really much bigger on the inside than I am on the outside."

That's it! What we need is not just a technique for management or a few new tricks to ensure efficiency. What we need in the business world today are managers and leaders who are bigger on the inside than they are on the outside. We need people whose inner qualities make them into people who elicit loyalty and commitment from their workers. We need leaders who inspire all of those around them with their vision and energy.

But what are those qualities, and how can we recognize the people who have them? What is even more important, how can we develop these traits in ourselves? In searching for a comprehensive list of the traits that are evident in those good people who elicit affectionate loyalty, there is no better source to which we can turn than the Bible. Even those who are not religious are likely to recognize that the Judeo-Christian Scriptures are a brilliant repository of truth when it comes to delineating what is good and right. For instruction in character building, the Bible is unrivaled. Down through the ages, the values which it prescribes have proven to be enduring and valid.

When W. C. Fields was old, sick, and near death, he was confined to a hospital bed. One day his wife, making an unexpected call on him, found him reading the Bible.

"W.C.!" she said with great surprise. "I can't believe you're reading the Bible. What's gotten into you?"

Fields, who was hardly a religious man, shot back in his sardonic voice, "Looking for loopholes, my dear . . . looking for loopholes."

Even old W.C. knew that the Bible was a solid book that speaks the truth for all people in all places and for all times. So it is to the Bible that we turn as we endeavor to ascertain what traits should be cultivated by the person who would have personal integrity. It is to the Bible that we turn when we want a list of those personal qualities that make someone good.

More specifically we focus in on Jesus, the Bible's main character. And when people asked Him to deal with the question of what constitutes the character of a truly good person, He answered:

> Thou shalt love the Lord thy God with all thy heart, and with all thy soul, and with all thy mind. This is the first and great commandment. And the second is like unto it, Thou shalt love thy neighbor as thyself.
>
> Matthew 22:37–39

It is *love.* According to Jesus, it is love for God and love for others that is the basis of all good character. People who love are good. People who do not love are not good. It is as simple as that.

The Bible goes on to define love for us, and its definition has come to be what many might call the best-known chapter in the New Testament—the thirteenth chapter of 1 Corinthians. (Note that I have included the appropriate equivalent for the King James "charity.")

> Though I speak with the tongues of men and of angels, and have not love, I am become as sounding brass, or a tinkling cymbal. And though I have the gift of prophecy, and understand all mysteries, and all knowledge; and though I have all faith, so that I could remove mountains, and have not love, I am nothing. And though I bestow all my goods to feed the poor, and though I give my body to be burned, and have not love, it profiteth me nothing. Love suffereth long, and is kind; love envieth not; love vaunteth not itself, is not puffed up, Doth not behave itself unseemly, seeketh not her own, is not easily provoked, thinketh no evil; Rejoiceth not in iniquity, but rejoiceth in the truth; Beareth all things, believeth all things, hopeth all things, endureth all things. Love never faileth: but whether there be prophecies, they shall fail; whether there be tongues, they shall cease; whether there be knowledge, it shall vanish away. . . . And now abideth faith, hope, love, these three; but the greatest of these is love.
>
> 1 Corinthians 13:1–8, 13

The messages in this Bible chapter are so packed with meaning that all of us—whether Jew, Christian, Muslim, or even atheist—can get a handle on what love is just by studying it. And that is exactly what we are going to do.

Love

I am a part of the Value of the Person team (VOP). This is a small group of people who are committed to improving labor-management relations for both large and small corporations across America. We have consulted with companies as big as 3M and General Motors, as well as with small firms such as Shaped Wire with its fifty employees.

Founded by Wayne Alderson, one-time CEO of Pitron Steel, the VOP team includes Reid Carpenter, president of the Pittsburgh Leadership Foundation, "Lefty" Scumanci, international director, Office, Technical, Professional Department, United Steelworkers of America, and myself. We conduct seminars that encourage labor and management to talk over ways to improve attitudes and behavior in the workplace.

VOP seminars, which take place over a two-day period, have proven to be incredibly successful in bringing about reconciliation and even friendship in the workplace between parties who have traditionally positioned themselves as enemies. While in no way sectarian or doctrinaire, the VOP team makes no apologies for its religious bias and makes spiritual renewal an integral part of what it sees as the hope for labor-management relations in the years to come.

Alderson teaches what he calls Theory R: Love, Dignity, and Respect. These, he contends, are attitudes and feelings that must be part of all relationships in the offices and factories of corporations if American business is to live up to its potential and be competitive in the world market.

VOP seminars are designed to expose ways in which the practices and policies of management have left workers feeling diminished and worthless, as well as to help the labor force to take a good look at the ways in which their attitudes and behavior have hurt and angered management.

What surprises me is that, after an initial period of defensiveness, genuine repentance usually sets in. A great deal of confession of sin takes place in these seminars—because *it is sin* to do things or treat people in ways that leave them dehumanized. Then there are long discussions as to how to change things and make the workplace into a good place. Promises made by both labor and management offer hope for genuine changes. Caring is expressed between individuals who have been adversaries.

I have yet to go through one of these seminars without seeing tears in the eyes of both sides. I have seen steelworkers and miners, who usually make a habit of putting on a macho bravado, break down as they tell the group how rotten they had been made to feel and how hateful this had made them act toward management. I have seen managers tell how they tried to be tough with the labor force because it was their only defense against the messages of contempt that they picked up from the workers.

What often seems like a cross between a sensitivity group session and a revival meeting seems to facilitate the breaking loose of a new honesty and openness between what had been warring parties. The interaction is both touching and promising. You cannot come away from a VOP seminar without a sense that there will be radical changes for the better in the workplace because of what has happened there.

My role in the VOP seminar program is to come in at the last session and talk about *love.* I try to explain what love is, how it is created, and how it can be expressed in both the home and the marketplace.

I believe that if I tried to introduce a discussion of love at the beginning of one of the seminars, I would be greeted with sneers and cynicism. But because the way has been prepared and both management and labor have had the chance to take off their masks and share their real feelings, the participants are ready.

What is unexpected is how hungry these people are for talk of love and how love can become an integral part of their lives in the workplace. Strange as it seems, laborers want bosses who *love* them. To be sure, they are unlikely to use the word *love.* Other words are employed. Words like *concern* and *willingness to listen* and *caring.*

At the close of one of the seminars, one manager actually made a verbal commitment to his work crew that from that day on he would remember each of them daily in prayer. He told a hushed audience that he always prayed for the people he loved because that was what his church had taught him to do. And if he was serious about loving those who were in that room with him, then he would make it a habit to pray for each of them regularly.

With an inquisitive sense of wonder, one of the workers responded, "Would you really do that for me?" He went on to explain, "I don't even believe in God, but if you pray for me every day I think I'm going to believe in you."

1 Corinthians 13 Restated

There are nine basic components of love outlined in the thirteenth chapter of 1 Corinthians, the great love chapter. These are traits which, if expressed, will establish you as a person of character. These are virtues which, if you live them out in the marketplace, will make you into the kind of person who will earn the respect of other people and what is even more important, will make you into the kind of person you, yourself, will respect. Verses 4–6 cite them clearly. They are:

Patience	=	Love suffereth long,
Kindness	=	and is kind;
Generosity	=	love envieth not;
Humility	=	love vaunteth not itself, is not puffed up,
Courtesy	=	doth not behave itself unseemly,
Unselfishness	=	seeketh not her own,
Good Temper	=	is not easily provoked,
Guilelessness	=	thinketh no evil;
Sincerity	=	rejoiceth not in iniquity, but rejoiceth in the truth;

Let us examine each of them and visualize how they might be played out in the business world. Let us see how well these biblically prescribed dispositions toward others will enable you to do good even as you, hopefully, do well in your factory or office.

Part 2

Love Is Work

6

Patience, Kindness, Generosity

As THE CHARACTERISTICS OF LOVE LISTED in 1 Corinthians 13 are examined, we find that *patience* is at the top of the list. "Love," says verse 4, "suffereth long."

Patience

Perhaps it seems strange to put patience in this number one slot. You may think that *self-sacrifice* or *steadfast affection* would be traits more deserving of this position. But, if you stop to think about it, patience provides a real revelation of how much you care about a person and how much you value a person at any given moment. You *may* claim to love a person without reservation, but how you *really* feel about him or her becomes blatantly clear when that person makes you wait. Your impatience makes the other person painfully aware that you have a condescending attitude.

Have you ever noticed how patient we can be with people who are famous or powerful or rich? When they are late or slow to meet our demands, those who are viewed as being above us on the stratification scales of life do not tick us off as do those whom we deem to be beneath us. We can be counted on to be patient when someone like a governor or a president is late. We smile and say that we understand. But when it comes to people whom we expect to serve us, we want immediate service and find waiting intolerable.

It is in this context that the apostle Paul writes:

> Let nothing be done through strife or vainglory; but in low-liness of mind let each esteem other better than themselves.
> Philippians 2:3

If each of us did this, none of us would be impatient and people around us would soon feel that we deem them to be of value. They might even think that we love them.

My job makes me into a frequent flyer on just about every airline in the country. It is a rare week that I escape the routine of going to the airport and hopping on a plane to go somewhere.

Airports, I find, are places where the true character of people really shows—particularly if there is some foul weather that causes planes to be grounded and flights canceled. On such occasions you can count on lines of angry and impatient people waiting for their respective turn to get at the ticket agent at the reservation desk.

Everyone knows that the options available are very limited. Nevertheless, there is a barrage of attacks on the unfortunate ticket agent. Person after person demands special treatment, as each tries to declare why he or she is more important than everyone else in line. The impatience that grows as these people are made to wait their turns is all too obvious, and the treatment of the ticket agent on such occasions is often brutal. There is arrogance in impatience, and you can almost sense these travelers saying, "How dare you treat me like this? Don't you know who I am? Don't you realize that I deserve special treatment?"

Every once in a while, someone steps up to the counter who radiates the kind of patience that Paul wrote about in 1 Corinthians 13. He or she seems to understand the plight of the ticket agent and may even offer words of consolation. The patience shown to the agent in such a hassled environment invariably comes as a desperately needed respite, and I love seeing a smile cross the once-stressed face. Score one for patience.

In the workplace a lack of patience is often seen when new assignments are given and those who are trying to learn what to do seem slow in picking up on what is expected of them. It is then that irritation, which too often goes hand-in-hand with impatience in such circumstances, commonly rears its ugly head.

I know an older woman who found it necessary to return to office employment after being deserted by her husband of twenty-eight years. The fears that she felt proved to be almost unbearable. She was not sure that she could still do what once had seemed to her to be easy.

Her first day in the office was a nightmare as she faced all the new equipment that twenty-eight years of technology had brought to the office scene. But nothing she had to face was as difficult as the impatience of the younger women who were her co-workers. They showed no patience with her, rolling their eyes if she asked for an explanation of something for the second time. They muttered under their breath when she became confused about using the computer. They complained constantly about having to take time to show her the location of basic items like paper supplies and postage stamps.

The story does not have a happy ending. The impatience of those younger women so unnerved my friend that she had to quit. Today she lives in poverty and is filled with self-doubt. She is a lonely person and depressed most of the time. Loving patience might have saved her.

Compare these stories with what a friend of mine experienced when he visited Dayspring, the L'Arche community for handicapped people in Toronto, Canada. He and his wife were there at the invitation of Henri Nouwen, the famous writer and one-time Harvard Divinity School faculty member.

Dr. Nouwen left all the academic glory of Harvard in order to join the staff of this center that provides care and ministry to special persons who, because they suffer severe physical, emotional, and mental handicaps, are incapable of caring for themselves. To many it seemed strange that this renowned scholar should spend his time with people who appear incapable of comprehending or appreciating his brilliance. But Dr. Nouwen is quick to point out that he is there not so much for what he can do for the people who are cared for at the center, but for what they can do for him.

It did not take long for my friend to experience for himself just what Dr. Nouwen was talking about. The "disabled" and intellectually slow residents of the community had enabled those who cared for them to learn to be patient. And through the process of learning patience, those who had come to serve had been introduced to some new and deeper dimensions of love.

The painstaking care that the men and women in the community required necessitated a slow, deliberate approach to every service rendered. These people could not and would not be rushed, and they required the total attention of those who cared for them.

At first my friend and his wife had difficulty in adjusting. They were active people who had "more important" things to do than just stand around, giving total attention to these "slow" people. But gradually they broke down. Little by little they were able to shut out the rest of the world and become completely involved with the people who had been entrusted to them for care.

My friends learned patience. Because in the end that's what love is. It is waiting for people as though they are all that matter. No wonder Paul placed patience first on his list of love's characteristics.

Are you patient in the office when you are trying to explain something and the other person does not quite get it?

Are you patient with those who work for you when they do not seem to be developing in the rapid fashion you expected?

Are you patient with people when they fail and ask for another chance?

Love is patient.

Love Is Kind

Kind people are committed to removing hurt. When someone is sad, the kind person empathizes and feels the hurt until the sadness of the other person is relieved. The kind person lives with a sensitive awareness of the pain others are enduring and seeks to comfort them. Love expresses itself in kindness, which means that the loving person is full of concern for the feelings of others.

I love the story a rabbi told me of the kindness of his father. One Sabbath on the way to the synagogue, his father said to him, "Samuel, slow down! Walk slowly! Do you see Mr. Blumenthal walking just ahead of us? He is getting very old and we do not want to pass him. Passing him will make him feel bad."

Kindness is trying to take into account how another person might feel as a consequence of what we do. Sometimes that consideration may force us to be "tough" in a present situation, because that is what a particular person needs in order to avoid great pain sometime in the future.

Take, as a case in point, a salesman in the insurance business who is constantly trying to impress people, especially clients, with his charm and his wit. But what the poor guy doesn't realize is that he has very bad breath. To tell him about his problem is to risk hurting his pride. But not to tell him is even more unkind. Sometimes the best expression of kindness is doing the tough thing.

Or consider what you should do about a romance developing in the office between a single secretary and her married boss. They have fooled themselves into thinking that nobody in the office knows what is going on. But in reality everybody knows. The gossip is running rampant, and it is only a matter of time before the word passes beyond the office, and a wife and children become painfully aware of what is happening to their husband and father.

The easiest course of action is to say nothing and to pretend that you haven't noticed the dangerous liaison that has been developing. You can even tell yourself that what they do is none of your business. Furthermore, if you confront the couple with what you know, he is likely to get angry. And then he might use his considerable influence to make trouble for you and hurt your possibilities for career advancement.

The risks are multiple and great. But if you do not do the tough thing, you will not do the kind thing. Kind people try to prevent hurt, and if you do not confront the couple, some innocent people are going to experience immeasurable pain.

When I asked why he did not tell me about this when I called for a recommendation, he said, "I felt sorry for him. I thought if he was given another chance, in another setting, things would work out for him and his wife. I did not want to ruin his future by telling you everything. It's not as though I lied. It's just that I thought there were some things better left unmentioned."

I am sure that this pastor thought he was being kind. But by doing what he did he was brutally unkind to many people, not the least of whom was the young man whom he was trying to convince himself that he was helping. Kindness is sometimes tough love in action.

Love Is Gracious

The Bible puts it in the negative. In this great love chapter we read, "love envieth not." The loving person can take pleasure in the good things that come to other persons. The awards and achievements of others are not begrudged. The loving person graciously shares in the joy of the good that others enjoy. There is no coveting in the loving person.

I know a preacher who tells of being invited to lead the closing prayer at a high school graduation in his township. He went and as he sat on the platform of the school auditorium to watch the ceremonies transpire, he noticed one graduating senior whose face radiated happiness. The secret of his happiness, it soon became apparent, was wrapped up in the fact that this boy seemed to be free of any trace of envy. He applauded wildly as the names of those who were receiving honors and awards were announced. As friends, one by one, received recognition for their requirement, he could not have been more pleased if he had received the awards himself. My friend added, "You know, at the end of the evening as the people mingled and the graduated students said their good-byes, it seemed as though that gracious boy was the only one who was completely happy. Most of the other graduates seemed to be a bit disappointed."

In life there is very little control over what recognition we receive from others. But each of us completely controls how we will react to the awards and recognitions that others receive.

And if we learn how to be happy when others are applauded then we can be sure that we can always be happy.

In the love chapter we read, "love envieth not!" When we love we can do what the young man at the graduation did. When we love we naturally know how to cheer the successes of others without any hint of envy.

7

Humility, Courtesy, Unselfishness

WHEN I WAS A BOY, I SAT IN CHURCH with my father on a Sunday when the preacher was expounding on the text, "Blessed are the meek, for they shall inherit the earth." When the text was read to the congregation, I heard my father mumble under his breath, "They'd better inherit it! It's the only way they'll get it."

Love Is Humble

Meekness and humility are hardly the traits that we usually think of looking for in those people who make things happen in the business world. Assertiveness is valued. Self-confidence is sought. It is the take-charge manner that gets high marks. Not that these traits are antithetical to humility, it is just that humility usually does not make it when we compile the list of character traits that make for success. In a workplace that requires tough negotiations, we gravitate toward the executive types who wear red "power" ties.

Humility is not what they teach in those success courses advertised in airline magazines. Yet if we really think about it, few character traits can earn as much respect as humility does when it comes to determining what we look for in a good leader. Those people who stand out as models are usually people who are noted for their humility. And few things are harder to take, particularly in especially competent people, than inflated egos.

Jesus offers a model of leadership that some have labeled servant leadership. There are obvious examples of His capacity for assertiveness, as can be seen in His readiness to stand up to the Pharisees and in His strong action against the money-changers in the temple (Matt. 21:12–13). But what truly symbolizes the character of Christ is His role as servant leader. When His disciples bickered among themselves as they vied for power positions, Jesus demonstrated what His kind of leaders were all about by washing their feet.

In the ancient world, it was the custom for the lowliest servant of a household to wash the feet of visitors. Walking on the unpaved roads of Israel meant that a traveler's feet were caked with dirt after a long journey. A good host always made provision for his guests by making sure that this menial and very necessary courtesy was provided.

None of the disciples were about to render this service. Each was too proud. Each was too concerned about losing status by assuming the role of servant. But Jesus, as the good leader, knew how to be a servant:

> He [Jesus] riseth from supper, and laid aside his garments; and took a towel, and girded himself. After that he poureth water into a basin, and began to wash the disciples' feet, and to wipe them with the towel wherewith he was girded.
> John 13:4–5

For those who want to be leaders, Jesus not only provides a crash course in humility, but He went on to teach His disciples the principles of servant leadership.

> If any man desire to be first, the same shall be last of all, and servant of all.
> Mark 9:35

True servanthood does not diminish a person's stature. Nor does true humility limit one's ability to exercise authority. In reality, the more that a leader demonstrates the capacity to be a humble servant, the more ability that leader will have to command the respect and allegiance of others.

As a case in point, let me recall the story about a drunk who was miraculously converted at a Bowery mission. Prior to his conversion, Joe had gained the reputation of being a hopeless, dirty wino for whom there was no hope, only a miserable existence in the ghetto. But following his conversion to a new life with God, everything changed. Joe became the most caring person that anyone associated with the mission had ever known. Joe spent his days and nights hanging out at the mission doing whatever needed to be done. There was never any task that was too lowly for Joe to take on. There was never anything that he was asked to do that he considered beneath him. Whether it was cleaning up the vomit left by some violently sick alcoholic or scrubbing the toilets after careless men left the men's room filthy, Joe did what was asked with a soft smile on his face and with a seeming gratitude for the chance to help. He could be counted on to feed feeble men who wandered into the mission off the street, and to undress and tuck into bed men who were too out of it to take care of themselves.

One evening, when the director of the mission was delivering his evening evangelistic message to the usual crowd of still and sullen men with drooped heads, there was one man who looked up, came down the aisle to the altar, and knelt to pray, crying out for God to help him to change. The repentant drunk kept shouting, "Oh God! Make me like Joe! Make me like Joe! Make me like Joe! Make me like Joe!"

The director of the mission leaned over and said to the man, "Son, I think it would be better if you prayed, 'Make me like *Jesus!*'"

The man looked up at the director with a quizzical expression on his face and asked, "Is he like Joe?"

Indeed, the first real communication of anything spiritual usually comes through people who demonstrate loving humility in the regular turn of daily events and especially in the rough spots of life. In the workplace it is possible for you and me to live out the humble spirit of Christ by showing respect for those tasks and responsibilities that others regard with condescension. To love is to deem no person an inferior and to value those who receive little recognition in the workplace. To act as though you are above others or to deem yourself too good for work that others must do is to incur deserved resentment. Thus Paul warns us in 1 Corinthians 13:4, "love vaunteth not itself, is not puffed up."

A good manager does not put himself or herself above the other workers. Instead, a good manager makes every employee aware of his or her importance and how much is depending on how well each job is done. Rather than striking fear into the workers by telling them that nobody's indispensable, a loving manager humbly elevates those who work under him or her by letting them know how essential they are. It was part of the mission of Jesus when here on earth to bring puffed-up big shots down a notch or two and to pick up those who had been relegated to the bottom of the organizational charts. His mother declared that mission in the Magnificat:

> He hath shewed strength with his arm; he hath scattered the proud in the imagination of their hearts. He hath put down the mighty from their seats, and exalted them of low degree.
> Luke 1:51–52

It is a good idea to learn something about humility, because the absence of this character trait in a manager can have dire consequences. But being humble has an even greater payoff. It is an important part of being the kind of loving person that you ought to be.

Love Is Courteous

Dr. James H. S. Bossard was a favorite teacher of mine in graduate school. During one of his lectures, I was whispering and joking in the back of the classroom with some of my classmates. As I look back upon it, I know I was being an obnoxious nuisance. Dr. Bossard, who knew that my vocational goal at that time was the Christian ministry, angrily demanded my attention and sternly said, "Mr. Campolo! You do not *have* to be a gentleman to be a clergyman, but it helps!"

The fact of the matter is, it does more than help. Courtesy is an essential expression of love. Loving people are instinctively courteous.

Samuel Taylor Coleridge considered the Scottish poet Robert Burns the finest gentleman he had ever known. Yet Burns had not been reared in the halls of the elite. He was not a member of the aristocracy. Instead "ole Bobby," as people loved to call him, was a simple man, born in a humble cabin just outside of the town of Ayr. But Burns was a loving man, and because he was a loving man he was *naturally* courteous.

Courtesy is a trait that is always found in loving people. That is because loving people have no desire to make others uncomfortable. Loving people always want others to feel special. Loving people are committed to making ordinary people feel like royalty. "Love," says the apostle Paul, "doth not behave itself unseemly."

When Peggy, my wife, was in high school, she worked one summer in the dress department of a discount clothing store. Finding neither the clothes nor the people very exciting, she decided to play a game. She would pretend she worked in Saks Fifth Avenue and that every woman looking for a dress was a charming, beautiful, and wealthy lady. From that day on she loved her job. Her daily activities became much more than a game. She enjoyed every customer because she gave her best—often to women who did not feel very good about either their appearance or the amount of money they had to spend. Peggy did incur some resentment because her commissions were higher than anyone else's! What she did because she is a loving person turned out to be good business that summer.

One of the most interesting stories about courtesy that I know comes from the life of Bishop Desmond Tutu, a Nobel Prize winner. As a boy he had learned the effects apartheid had upon the ways in which black people were treated by white people. Indignities were to be expected, and humiliation was felt in most encounters with "superiors."

But one day as the young Tutu was walking down the street with his mother, they confronted a white Anglican clergyman. Unexpectedly, the Anglican priest stepped aside in a deferring manner and tipped his hat at the boy's mother, showing her uncommon courtesy.

Young Tutu was very surprised at the courtesy that had been shown to his mother. He turned to her and asked, "Why was that white man so nice to you?"

"That man is a minister of the gospel," his mother answered. "People like that are courteous to everyone."

Bishop Tutu remembers saying to himself there and then that he wanted to be an Anglican priest.

Courtesy in the workplace is always evident among those who would be loving. If you have chosen to become the kind of person who reflects a Christlike character, you cannot help but want to learn how to do those things that will enhance the sense of dignity of those with whom you work nine to five.

When I hear secretaries complain about having to get their bosses coffee, I am immediately aware that there is something far deeper that is bothering them. I sense that the real issue is that they feel that their humanity is diminished by the *way* in which they are asked to get coffee. The actual act is no big deal to most of them. Rather, it is usually the sum total of the indignities that they have to endure day in and day out to which they are reacting when they object to getting coffee. Sometimes these indignities become obscene because of sexual harassment. When people *need* their jobs, they often end up enduring "arrows of outrageous fortune."

Secretaries are sometimes treated as nonpersons whose only reason to exist is to cater to their bosses' whims. As anyone who has ever worked in an office knows, one good secretary is worth two or more junior executives. But salary scales too often do not reflect the real value of a good secretary to the organization or executive he or she serves.

Courtesy changes everything. When a female secretary is not referred to as "the girl who works for me" and has a name and proper ascription, the tension and discontent usually disappear. When secretaries are politely *asked* to carry out assignments instead of *ordered* to do so, attitudes become more positive. "Please" is something many office managers have never learned to say.

Perhaps one of the practices that has to be considered as

we think about the problems associated with courtesy, or the lack thereof, is the dress code we follow. Dress is a statement. In our ego-centered society we have come to think of dress as something that we do to attract attention to ourselves. We dress in order to impress people. But courteous persons do not so much dress to enhance their own images as they do to enhance those around them. They dress to make others feel good and comfortable about themselves.

If I came to the office in sloppy dress, I might be saying to those I work with, "I really don't care very much about you. I certainly am not about to dress up for you as I would if I were going to meet somebody important." What you wear tells those you work with how you rate them.

If people dress like slobs, the effects on themselves and those around them are more than obvious. It is no wonder that elitist prep schools, which are designed to turn out young men and women with manners, always have dress codes.

On the other hand, it can be just as offensive to overdress. What you wear should not make others around you feel inferior. If it does, dress becomes a "put down." Overdressing can demonstrate a lack of love. It is something that people who "behaveth unseemly" might do.

Love Is Unselfish

In the love chapter, we read, "Love seeketh not her own." That means that love is not selfish. Or, in language that relates to what goes on in the everyday activities of the workplace, loving people do not always insist on having things their way.

This particular attribute of a loving person very much flies in the face of the advice in most of the books about how to improve self and sales in the business world. Just considering the titles of such books will give you some idea of how contrary to love they are:

The Art of Selfishness
Winning with Deception and Bluff
Winning Through Intimidation
Creative Aggression

Recently I was at a sales conference in which the speaker was pressing audience members to go out into the marketplace with a clear image in mind as to what things each of them would buy with their commissions. He was eloquent and persuasive but, to my way of thinking, completely immoral. Having been impressed with some of the ideas being promoted by the New Age movement, he had taken to heart the belief that "imaging" things has the capacity to motivate people to make having these things a reality. I can still hear him saying: "Get a clear image of that Jaguar or Mercedes. Or perhaps it's a trip to Hawaii that is high on your list of wants. Before you go to see that prospect, get a clear picture of what you will buy with your commission. Think how much you want it. Taste it! And then go in and get that client to help you get it!"

In all of that, there was only self-interest. There was no concern for what the client needed or wanted. There was not even consideration of whether or not the client could afford to buy what was being sold.

Love is not this way. Love wants to be sure that the client is still a friend in the future, when all the factors are known.

The other night I saw "20/20"'s Barbara Walters interview with Seema Boesky, former wife of the infamous Wall Street insider trader, Ivan Boesky. As this hurt woman told her story and explained how her husband had operated, it became starkly clear how incredibly self-centered he had been. He had used everyone—from his employees and friends to his own wife—to get what he wanted. And when he was finally caught in his crime, he did not hesitate to betray his friends and associates if doing so might in any way contribute to a lighter sentence for him.

It was clear that Ivan Boesky had always been a man who selfishly looked after his own interests with little or no concern for others. He was the man caricatured by Michael Douglas in the movie *Wall Street*. And it was from Boesky's own words that Douglas took off in the speech on greed that made seeing the movie a "must" for MBA students. In that speech, greed is praised as a virtue that makes the capitalistic system work. Greed is described as the fuel that fires the engines of industry. It is considered the motivation for investments and the driving force behind productive efficiency.

Humility, Courtesy, Unselfishness

That kind of self-interested greed stands in diametrical opposition to what love requires of people. Love is certainly not opposed to making profits from ingenuity and labor, but it never allows a person to exploit others on the way to success. Love can never be selfish.

Most of us are not like the wheeler-dealers on Wall Street represented by the likes of Ivan Boesky. For most of us, the fight against selfishness is waged in the daily negotiations that go on in the office and in the shop. Our battles against selfishness deal with such concerns as who gets the office with the view and who gets the best desks and chairs. It is in those meetings where you want all the decisions to go your way and to serve your interests—regardless of how it affects others—that selfishness and love do battle within you. Love does not mean that you let yourself be pushed around or run over by others. It simply demands that decisions be made with everybody's interest in mind.

A tuba player in a concert band cut his lip and was unable to play his horn. For the first time in years he was in the audience listening to the music while another player took his place on stage. After the concert someone asked him what it was like being a listener instead of a performer. He answered, "It was wonderful! I had forgotten that the whole band wasn't playing 'Um-pah-pah'!"

It is easy to get so caught up in the part that you yourself are playing that you all but forget about the needs of the others with whom you work. The smallest package in the world is a person all wrapped up in him or herself. And it is love that can keep us from being that kind of person.

8

A Good Temper, Guilelessness, Sincerity

THOSE WHO HAVE COMMITTED THEMSELVES to being persons whose character is marked by love are, says the apostle Paul, "not easily provoked." They do not easily lose their temper. They are able to keep their cool when things go wrong, and they are not likely to get angry at people who sometimes fail to do what is expected of them.

Love Has a Good Temper

Stop to consider that we really do not lose our tempers. We say that we do, but in reality we only choose to fly off the handle with certain people. There are others, who matter to us more, with whom we would never lose our tempers. It is unlikely that many people lose their tempers in personal discussions with the president of the United States. We do not lose our tempers with those *whose love and/or support we are afraid to lose.*

You are not likely to lose your temper with someone you are dating if that person is extremely desirable to you and is also interested in dating others. You wait until the person is "secured" or married to you. Then you tell yourself that you have the right to blow up because you think it is safe to do so.

In the office, you are not likely to lose your temper with the person who, at the moment, is absolutely essential and ir-replaceable—and who has other job options. Instead, you tend to lose your temper with those who are, on the one hand, dis-pensable, and who, on the other hand, are greatly dependent upon keeping their jobs in order to meet the basic needs of their lives. We are usually more careful not to lose our tempers with people whose poor opinions of us could ruin our reputations among important friends and associates. However, this does not keep the word about a bad-tempered person from getting out into those circles where it can do him or her harm and even di-minish possibilities for advancement. The effects of losing one's temper, even with those whom one perceives as an underling, may have far greater consequences than most people can pre-dict. The little people you yell at today may do you in tomor-row. So be careful even if you do not opt to be kind.

The real reason to keep your temper under control does not lie in the pragmatic results of self-control. Instead it is some-thing that love requires. Loving people have nothing to do with the kind of intimidation that losing one's temper is usually aimed at creating. Love has no desire to see people cowed or made afraid. As a matter of fact, "perfect love casteth out fear" (1 John 4:18).

Love Is Guileless

Loving people do not impute evil motives to others; "Love thinketh no evil." My wife is that kind of person. She always thinks the best of people. She never figures that anyone's intentions are evil. She always regards strangers with the confidence that they are basically good people who can be trusted.

Of course, this lets her in for all kinds of ripoffs. She gets taken from time to time by con artists. But she tells me that she would rather be "had" occasionally than to go around being suspicious of every person she meets.

We travel a great deal, and one time we were in a small impoverished community in Mexico. Peggy had written a stack of postcards. She went to the post office to buy stamps, but the man behind the counter told her they were out of the ones she needed. He offered to take her cards and the money and to put stamps on the cards and mail them for her later. So Peggy, trusting soul that she is, gave him the money to mail the many cards she had written.

When she later joined me and told me about what she had done, I could only sigh cynically and tell her that she could say good-bye to both the money and the cards. I let Peggy know that I was sure that the man to whom she had given her money and postcards could not be trusted. And she let me know that she had no reason to believe that the man at the post office was anything but an honest and trustworthy person.

Sadly, Peggy was wrong and I was right. The postcards were never received by her friends and relatives. "That's okay," she later told me. "I would rather be cheated now and then than go through life not trusting people. I don't see how people can go on living if they distrust everyone they meet."

Of course, my wife is right, even if it means getting stung from time to time. It is a heavy burden to go around thinking evil of everyone you meet.

You have to feel sorry for that person in the office who sees evil motives in everything that everybody else in the place does on a given day. There is the junior executive who sees the whole office in political terms and figures that everybody is trying to sabotage his career so that they do not have to compete with him for promotions and raises. Whenever someone is nice to him, he asks himself, "What's he up to? Why is she being nice to me?"

This poor guy is unable to take any gesture of kindness at face value. He is always looking for some diabolical motive behind any gift or act of kindness.

Of course, we all know that the person who "thinketh evil" of another is practicing what the psychologists call projection. People tend to impute to others their own character. If they are evil and conniving, they assume that everybody else is the same way. If they are out to make the people in the office who are vying with them for higher positions look bad in the eyes of the boss, they will assume that others are, likewise, trying to do them in.

On the other hand, those who are loving and good will always expect others to be just as loving and just as good as they are. That is what Paul is telling us in 1 Corinthians 13:5, when he writes that "love thinketh no evil."

There is an ancient Chinese story about an old sage who was walking along a highway when he was met by a traveler walking in the opposite direction. The traveler asked, "Sir, seeing that you have just come from the city to which I am traveling, can you tell me what kind of city it is? Is it a good and happy city?"

"What was it like in the city from which you came?" inquired the old sage.

"It was a terrible place," the traveler answered. "It was dirty and the people were gross and stupid. It had odors that made me cringe. There is not one good thing that I could say about it."

"I am sorry to have to tell you that the city to which you are traveling is much the same," answered the sage. "It is everything that you did not like in the city you left behind."

The sage continued his journey. In time, he met a second traveler who asked him the same question. "Can you tell me about the city to which I am traveling? Is it a good place to live? Will I be happy there?"

Again the sage asked, "What was it like in the city from which you have just come?"

"Oh, it was a wonderful place. The people were kind and good. The buildings were beautiful. It was the happiest place I have ever been."

"Then I have good news for you," answered the sage. "The city to which you are traveling is exactly the same!"

The old sage knew that what people *are* determines what they find in cities and in other people. Those who are evil think that everything and everyone around them is evil. But those who love "thinketh no evil."

Impute good motives to others! Think the best of others! Believe in people! Even if you lose now and then, you ultimately win. It is better to lose out from time to time while maintaining an attitude that ultimately wins. It is a cynical attitude toward people that will ultimately make you into a loser. Go with love.

"Love," says the apostle Paul, "never fails." And love "thinketh no evil."

Love Is Sincere

I find that some office talk, particularly certain kinds of humor, can be worse than offensive. It is possible for talking to be downright evil. The kinds of jokes that are exchanged at the water cooler and the things that get talked about during coffee breaks can be racist, sexist, and otherwise mean.

Loving people will have no part of such talk. They find pleasure in hearing good things. And they let it be known that talk that runs people down or hurts others is not welcomed. Loving people get no pleasure out of hearing about the failures of others nor any joy in exposing the shortcomings of others. Loving people are never found in the despicable group that gloats over the news that dirt has been uncovered about another.

In 1 Corinthians 13:6, we read that love "rejoiceth not in iniquity, but rejoiceth in the truth." And that says it all.

Shortly after the scandals surrounding the lives of Jim Bakker and Jimmy Swaggart made national headlines, I was a speaker for a pastors' conference. The clergy at this gathering were very much enjoying the commonly circulated jokes about these fallen televangelists. They exhibited a kind of self-righteous superiority that I found very hard to take. There was some obvious pleasure among them in having witnessed the fall of these two men who, in so many ways, now seemed to be a contradiction to the gospel they had preached.

When it was time for me to speak, I started off by saying, "We ought to be careful what we say about Jim Bakker and Jimmy Swaggart since the only difference between them and the rest of us, is that they haven't found out about the rest of us yet."

No, I did not think that my clergy audience were people who had had sex with prostitutes. Maybe some had; I just do not think so. But I am sure that if all of the ugly secrets of our past were to become public knowledge, not many of us would be able to survive the public disgrace.

In Philippians 4:8 the apostle Paul gives careful directions that should govern what we say and think in our relationships with others:

> Whatsoever things are true, whatsoever things are honest, whatsoever things are just, whatsoever things are pure, whatsoever things are lovely, whatsoever things are of good report; if there be any virtue, and if there be any praise, think on these things.

This is good instruction, not only for the workplace but for every situation in life.

In the business world, false flattery seems to be a habit. Time and time again I hear from people who tell me that they were complimented and *told* that their work was just fine, only to find that a few days or weeks later they were "let go" because their work was unacceptable. Insincere compliments always end up hurting.

In sales, insincerity can reach epidemic levels. At times we're almost taught to be insincere. We laugh at jokes that are offensive. We smile in the face of what we disapprove. And we pretend to really "like" people. All to get them to sign on the dotted line. In Haiti, I attended a conference that brought together both American missionaries and indigenous pastors. The Americans were inquisitive about how to gain acceptance in the communities where they had established their ministries. They wanted to know from the Haitian pastors just what it was that would enable them to be trusted by the local people.

After a long silence, one of the pastors spoke. "Missionaries always tell us that they love us. Yet they do not show their love. At least they do not do what we would expect from someone who loves us. But there was one missionary who loved us, and we were sure that he did. When one of the men of my village died of a heart attack he came to the house and stayed with the family all day and all night. That is what people who are sincere in their love do for my people."

The missionary referred to in the story happened to be present and said, "I did not realize that it was that significant a thing. I just thought the family needed me."

Of course, that is the point. Love is sincere, and sincerity is when actions agree with voiced statements.

Restating 1 Corinthians 13 for the Office

Irenaus, one of the early Church Fathers, once said, "With love there are no questions. Without love there are no answers." The truth of that statement is effectively verified in the daily activities of the business world. Living out love in relationships with employees, associates, and clients will impact all of these relationships in the best possible ways and lead to the only kind of success that has lasting significance. And without love? Well, let me paraphrase the great love chapter in response to that question.

> Although I have the communication skills of men and of angels, and have not love, I am nothing but a sounding brass or a clanging cymbal. And if I can predict marketing trends and have a total grasp of production techniques, and although I have the kind of positive thinking that can-do people say is the secret of success and have not love, it really does no lasting good. And although I make all the sacrifices so that there can be better wages for my workers, and make sure that they have all the fringe benefits possible and do not show them love, it will still leave them grumbling and discontented. Love teaches me to put up with a lot of things that would ordinarily make me angry, and it makes me into a listening, sensitive person. It keeps me from acting like a big shot and going on ego trips. Love keeps me from being rude to even the lowliest worker in the company. It keeps me from always demanding that things be done my way; it keeps me from blowing up at the least little thing. And it prevents me from keeping files on all the mistakes made by people under me. Love gets no satisfaction out of the failures of others—even when their failures guarantee that I will get a promotion.

9

A Word from the Unions

SERVING, AS I DO, AS PART OF A CONSULTING team that works on labor/management relationships, I often have the opportunity to talk to union leaders. I get to hear about their hopes and their frustrations. I get to hear about their joys and their hurts. And I also learn from them what character traits they look for in those who occupy positions of leadership.

Over and over again, union leaders cite two virtues as being essential in good management. Above all else, they look for *trustworthiness* and *fairness* in their bosses. They want to deal with employers whose word can be trusted. And they want to be sure that *everybody* who is in the union gets justice from those who govern the workplace.

Being as Good as Your Word

I suppose that if you really stop to think about it, having those with whom you work believe in you as a person of your word is something that most of us want very much. To be viewed by others as a man or woman of integrity is not only personally desirable, but of integral importance in the workplace. And if, in your dealings with people, you ever lose your integrity, you will not only have lost what is a very precious character trait, but you will have lost an essential requisite of an effective leader.

The Baptist church my family attended during my growing-up years had a church covenant that the congregation read in unison on the first Sunday of each month when we celebrated holy communion. Hearing it over and over as I did, I committed much of it to memory and the following words made a lasting impression on me:

I will be faithful in all my obligations and engagements. I will be slow to anger and always ready for reconciliation.

These are good words for a growing child to hear regularly repeated. And they are good words for a manager or worker to consider daily.

I live close to the Amish community of Lancaster County, Pennsylvania. These austere descendants of the Anabaptist movement commonly known as the Pennsylvania Dutch, have earned the desirable reputation of being people of character. Their word can be trusted, and whatever they promise they will deliver.

The Amish refuse to sign written contracts because they contend that, as Christians, their word should be good enough to guarantee any agreement that is sealed with a shake of the hand. In accord with biblical directives, they feel that there is no need for anything more. Certainly, there should be absolutely no need for any kind of oath. The word of Christians, they contend, should not need any reinforcement. As Jesus said in the Sermon on the Mount,

Let your communication be, Yea, yea; Nay, nay: for whatsoever is more than these cometh of evil.
Matthew 5:37

Unfortunately, very few organizations function with the high character standards of the Amish. I regularly encounter men and women who have been left hurt and disillusioned because of their experiences in the business world. Broken contracts and failed obligations seem to be evident everywhere. The business world seems to be filled with those who are ready to go back on agreements and disappoint expectations if it means a more profitable bottom line for them.

An insurance company was recently bought out by a competitor. In order to encourage the staff to go along with the merger, those in management assured the employees that they would enjoy the same pay and benefits under their new managers that they had under the former owners. But, following the merger, the employees found out that their pension program would not be continued after the merger. This would leave many of the workers in precarious circumstances following retirement. Unfortunately, by the time the office workers realized what was going on, it was too late.

They had been betrayed. The word of their former employers was not to be trusted. Unfortunately, these workers had to find out the hard way.

Broken promises litter the organizational landscape along with the broken lives they create. How many people have left good jobs in response to the promises of great opportunities that never materialized? How many junior executives have allowed themselves to be exploited and have made great personal sacrifices because they were led to believe that they were in line for promotions, only to have their hopes dashed by employers who passed over them and gave the prized positions to others.

My daughter, Lisa, who is a lawyer, has told me of young associates who slave long hours because they have been made to believe that they are on their way to becoming partners in their law firms. She tells me, "It's not being turned down in the quest for partnership that hurts most young lawyers. It's that they were led to believe that partnership was a certainty if they just would keep up the good work."

When employers leave workers disillusioned, often it is not because of anything that they specifically and explicitly say or do. In most cases, the painful disillusionment comes from what is implied or what has been implicit in discussions. Those who are guilty of misleading their employees can usually say with an air of righteous indignation, "But I never really *said* that I would do what you suggest or *promised* what you seem to think that I did."

True! But what is *implied* can be used to manipulate people, and what is implicit can often get people to make significant sacrificial changes in their lives.

I wish I could say that it is just within the dog-eat-dog businesses of the secular community that untrustworthiness is to be found. But to be really frank, deception and the resulting disillusionment seems even more common in the world of non-profit institutions, and especially in religious organizations. Even among Christian missionary societies there are reports of betrayal and disillusionment. This is particularly likely to happen when the person who is doing the hiring is a visionary.

Sometimes a visionary, charismatic leader inspires people who are more down to earth to envision what might be with such force that these followers assume that the "*might* be" is a sure thing, guaranteed to become reality. The unsuspecting follower believes absolutely that, in the very near future, he or she will be in a position to do incredibly important work for God with a solid basis of financial support. When fewer funds than were envisioned are delivered or become reality, the disappointment proves overpowering. This sort of thing has led some to lose faith not only in a charismatic leader and an organization, but, what is far worse, in God Himself.

Fair Is Fair

Fairness is the other virtue that I find union leaders most want to find in management. Many contend that they have to keep a constant eye on what management does. They say that anything less than careful vigilance on their part would result in management sneaking in changes in policy and practice that would mean unfair treatment for the workers. The union leaders that I have met are suspicious of management and, usually, for good reason.

Fair is the common word for "justice" in the marketplace. A sense of fairness is what people have when they feel that they're being treated right by those who are above them. Children demand it from their parents and are incensed if they do not get it. Nothing makes a child feel more unloved than suspicion that parents favor a brother or sister. A child studies everything that parents mete out to siblings and screams with outrage if there is any sign that he or she has been slighted or in any way expected to live up to standards that don't apply to the rest of the family. A child constantly compares the treatment he or she receives from parents with what the others in the family receive. There is often gloating on the part of the one perceived as being the favorite. And a seething anger rises in the one who feels that the parents are harder on him or her than on brothers and sisters. When a child cries out, "That's not fair!" what is really being said is, "You don't love me as much." For children, fairness is the ultimate demand.

At school the same cry is heard. The complaints of students are seldom about the quality of the education being offered or about the competence of teachers. Their complaints always seem to be about fairness. Students of all ages complain that the grading is not fair, the rules are not fair, the work load is not fair . . . the list of grievances seems to have no end, as any dean of students knows all too well.

Of course, the call for fairness is carried into the workplace, and those in business who are known as being persons of character always demonstrate an exceptional capacity for fairness. Fairness is the just treatment that those who wield power and prestige in an organization dispense to those who are beneath them. It is something that those who lack the power to make the daily decisions that affect them in the marketplace expect from the men and women who are above them. Those who get treated unfairly usually have little recourse to address the unjust treatment they receive. They seldom have the chance even to complain. In most instances, the victims of unfairness feel humiliated as each says inwardly, "There's nothing I can do about it."

John Perkins, one of this country's outstanding African-American leaders, tells a story out of his childhood which provides brilliant insight into what is involved subjectively when a person is treated unfairly in the workplace. He says:

> I was about eleven years old when I got a powerful lesson in economics. It was a lesson which helped me see why poor families like mine stayed poor while the rich got richer.

I stood on a farmer's back porch, waiting for him to come back with the money. I was bone-tired, that good kind of tired that comes after a hard day's work. The kind of tired a boy earns from doing a man's worth of hauling on a hot, humid summer day in Mississippi.

But if my body was remembering the day's work, my mind was flying ahead to what I could do with the dollar or dollar and a half that would soon be in my pocket. Would I buy a shiny new pocket knife? That would really wow the guys back home. Or what about a wallet?

Not that I really needed these things, you see. But I *was* a few miles away from home. For kids in our town that was big stuff. Vacations were always an occasion for bragging— so much so that the kids who did not go on vacations had to invent them.

So that's how this thing got started, this custom of buying something while you're gone to prove where you've been. What you bought wasn't all that important. What was important was what it would prove.

The farmer came through the kitchen on to the back porch. I held out my hand expectantly. Into it fell—I could hardly believe it—just two coins. A dime and a buffalo nickel! I stared into my hand. If that farmer would have knocked the wind out of me, I couldn't have been any more surprised . . . or hurt . . . or humiliated.

I had been used. And I couldn't do a single thing about it. Everything about it was wrong—everything in me wanted to throw that blasted money on the floor and stomp out of there.

But I couldn't. I knew what white people said about "smart niggers." I knew better than to be one of those.

I shuffled off that back porch, head down—ashamed, degraded, violated. I didn't want anyone to know I had been exploited. I hated myself.

Among young and old alike the kind of indignities that John Perkins endured at the hands of that white Mississippi farmer are all too familiar. Many of us in the dominant white society have been stung by the accusations of unfairness that have been hurled at us by the spokespersons of the African-American community. Undoubtedly we deserve these harsh condemnations. Even if we were not the ones who were guilty of the unfair treatment of those of other races who worked, or tried to work, alongside us in business and industry, so often we had little, if anything, to say as we watched others put them down. Our conspiracy of silence permitted oppression and made repentance and retribution necessary in order to create a new sense of fairness. Our lack of character in these matters has justified those who speak against us!

The political attempt to restore fairness in the marketplace for minority peoples has been Affirmative Action programs. Mandated by government decree, institutions and businesses across the country have been required to give evidence that they are giving employment opportunities to minority people in proportion to the percentage of each minority group in the general population of the community.

In simple language, Affirmative Action means a quota system. In its most explicit form, referred to as the Philadelphia Plan, Affirmative Action means that a company doing business with the government must show that the proper number of minority people are present in the work force or else the government contracts with the company are rendered null and void.

Personally, I think that Affirmative Action programs were a good idea that may have outlived their usefulness. When originally implemented, they forced a rapid redress of the unfairness that had been suffered by minority peoples. But over the past few years, Affirmative Action has often resulted in reverse discrimination. There are increasing numbers of cases where white workers with superior qualifications have been refused employment simply because hiring them would prevent the employers from meeting the prescribed quotas for minorities laid down by law.

In the face of this reverse discrimination, people of character should stand up for fairness for all people and, within the organizations where they work, they should strive to see to it that the most deserving workers get promotions, regardless of race or background.

10

The Case for Special People

OVER THE LAST FEW YEARS ALL OF US HAVE become aware of the unfair treatment that women have been forced to endure in the workplace. Prejudices against women have kept them out of certain jobs and prevented them from rising to the top positions in many organizations. Women often talk about a glass ceiling that they bump into as they endeavor to move up the corporate ladder.

Complaints from Women

Companies often find it desirable to hire women. Having women in the lower levels of management within a corporation portrays the right kind of open and liberal image. Besides, Affirmative Action guidelines require treating women as a minority group deserving preference in hiring policies. However, once employed, women often complain that they are treated unfairly within the system. They claim that their bosses limit the positions to which they can realistically aspire.

I have talked with employers about this complaint, and I have been somewhat surprised by their candid responses on the subject. One of them said, "It's all good and well to say we ought to give women the same chances as men, but you ought to face the consequences of this fact—men don't get pregnant and women do."

I knew what he was driving at. In the mission organization I lead, women hold most of the key leadership positions. A number of times pregnancies have removed key women, and in each case our entire organization has experienced a major setback. In the late stages of pregnancy and in those periods immediately following childbirth, those female executives were unable to do their work. Others had to fill in for them and try to carry out some very difficult and complex tasks. Not only did this overtax the rest of those in the office, but the efficiency of the organization in certain areas decreased dramatically.

Furthermore, many *women* are claiming that it is naive to believe that a woman can be a mother and a top executive at the same time. The demands of each of these roles pulls the woman away from the other. When she's at work, her mind is partly on her child. And when she's at home with her child, her mind is often back at the office.

The arguments against female executives who become mothers are not easily dismissed. On the other hand, might not the problem be in the way we have structured things in our society? While it is true that the woman becomes pregnant, it is not true that only she is a parent. Where is her husband? By what right does his life go on unchanged following the birth of his child while his wife is expected to significantly alter hers? *That just doesn't seem fair!*

I am not suggesting that a child be put in day care, which is usually what happens to the children of working mothers. In reality I am not convinced that day care is as healthy socially or psychologically for children as being reared at home by parents (and I can produce empirical studies to back up that claim). What I *am* suggesting is that caring for a child ought to be a shared responsibility. A child *does* interrupt careers if both parents are aspiring executives. But fairness suggests that, in such cases, having a child ought to interrupt the careers of fathers just as much as it interrupts the careers of mothers. If this were the case, then employers would face almost the same difficult considerations when hiring a man as they face when hiring a woman.

Things are changing. When I was a new father I was somewhat detached from the role of caring for my children. My son, who has recently become a father, is much more involved. He does not put in as many hours of daily childcare as does his wife, since it is her choice to make motherhood her full-time career at this time, but my son does carry his fair share of the responsibility of parenthood in a way that I did not. I wish that I had done better and would like to think I would be more like my son if I had another chance.

When I consider the disruptions to my own organization that have resulted because of the pregnancies of some of our top women leaders, I have to admit that many of them occurred primarily because we were not organized to make allowances for such things. These women were doing such a fantastic job that I never wanted to consider the possibility of having to do without them for even a few weeks. Looking back on it all, I must admit that had we planned better we could have established a system that would have carried the organization through those pregnancies with a minimum of difficulty. And to those who might ask, "Why go through all this trouble?" I answer, "Because it's fair."

Unfair wages for Women

I am not sure that it will come as much of a surprise when I tell you that, according to most studies, women get paid only 70 percent of what men get paid for doing the same work. Actually one of the reasons for the "success" of American capitalism has been the *unfair* wages and salaries paid to women.

There are those who would argue that women ought to be paid less since, in most cases, they are not the primary breadwinners of their families. In reality any such statement is far removed from the real situation. Just about half of all children in America are presently being raised in single-parent homes. And, in an overwhelming number of cases, these single-parent homes are headed up by mothers. Second, in our capitalistic society, payment is not made on the basis of people's needs. Actually, I wish that such were the case, because it would end the suffering and privation experienced by millions of families across this country. Supposedly, in America, salaries and wages are meted out in accordance with the level of the job, the unique skill of the worker, his or her seniority on the job, and the value of the work done to the company. This being the case, wage discrimination on the basis of gender or need is wholly unfair.

God's Invisible Minority

The young man sat in my office. There were beads of perspiration on his brow. He was fidgeting with a ballpoint pen, and he seemed sufficiently distraught to be heading for a nervous breakdown. He was a homosexual and the man with whom he had had an affair more than a decade ago was about to expose him.

This young man's one-time friend belonged to a group that believed that homosexuals who remain "in the closet" hurt the Gay Rights movement. This group was making a practice of forcing those who wanted to keep their homosexual orientation secret to reveal who and what they really were.

"I'll lose my job!" he told me. And there were tears in his eyes.

"I work for the government, and my boss has let it be known that homosexuals have no place in government work."

At this point I must make my own case on behalf of those with homosexual orientations. While I believe that the Bible explicitly condemns homosexual behavior, I am amazed by the fact that many of my churchgoing friends have great difficulty distinguishing between orientation and behavior. This book is not the place for me to go into a long discussion about whether homosexual orientations are inborn or have social origins, but I do know that those with homosexual orientations do not *choose* to be the way they are any more than heterosexuals choose their orientations. Whatever imprints a person's thinking patterns into a homosexual orientation occurs before that person even knows what is going on.

In the matter of homosexuals in the secular workplace, I contend that if they keep their sex lives private and go about their work with proper efficiency and decorum, then it is unfair to discriminate against them. Discrimination on the basis of sexual orientation is certainly not what I would expect from persons of character. What is more, I think that it is a very negative testimony to the world at large if a Christian allows his or her religious convictions to become the basis for unfair discrimination.

Fairness requires that a Christian employer in the secular workplace not impose his or her personal religious convictions on others. It just is not fair that those employed in a company which does not legally designate itself as a religious organization should have to conform in their personal lives outside the company to expectations of employers who happen to be evangelical Christians.

What Should Those Who Lead Christian Organizations Expect from Homosexuals?

A religious organization (defined as such by the legal status it enjoys with the IRS) is justified in handling the matter of employing homosexuals somewhat differently. And it is here that the difference between homosexual orientation and homosexual behavior becomes very important. While a Christian organization may find it necessary not to employ people involved in homosexual *behavior,* it is still quite wrong to discriminate on the basis of homosexual *orientation.*

In a Christian organization, if a person is willing to *behave* according to the requisites of the Bible, even though he or she might have inclinations to behave otherwise, then that person should be welcomed to share as a partner in the organization's mission. After all, if we threw out everyone who had a strong *temptation* to violate biblical regulations, who would be left? Not even Jesus would be employable, because He was tempted in *all* ways like we are tempted—though He never once sinned.

Why we are tempted or inclined to sin is not what should matter in religious organizations. What should be important is what people believe and do. However (and this is a *big* "however"), if a homosexual decides to live out his or her sexual desires, then that is another story. No religious organization can be expected to allow persons in their employment to live out a sexual lifestyle that conflicts with the message and vision for society which it is trying to promote. The leader of a religious organization, *in fairness to the contributors* who keep the organization going, must maintain integrity and see to it that those who are employed try to live out the values which the organization is about.

The missionary organization that I lead has had at least two young men with homosexual orientations work with us. In both cases, these men claimed to have struggled with their sexual orientations and had come to accept who and what they were. However, each of them, as a committed evangelical Christian was convinced that homosexual *behavior* was contrary to the teachings of Scripture, and therefore off-limits for them. They served Christ and our mission program well. While homosexual behavior would not have been tolerated, I considered it fair that these two young men be allowed to serve as missionaries with us.

I have gone through this discussion of homosexuals in the workplace, not only because it is becoming more and more of an issue, but to show that sometimes doing the fair thing may require that religious persons take a stand *against* some of the opinions that prevail in their churches. Such a stand may even disturb some of the other workers in their organizations, but fair people hang tough about what is right.

In my own Christian missionary organization, I was once questioned by one of my board members about the two celibate homosexual men who were serving with our staff. When I confirmed that his suspicions about their orientations were true, he resigned in a huff and took his annual financial contribution with him. Being fair can be costly.

On the other hand, none of the co-workers of these two young men ever questioned whether or not they should be on our staff. It was obvious to those who knew them well that each of them did his best to live according to God's Word and to behave "circumspectly" in the world.

How Fairness Is Judged

The test of your own fairness is how you are viewed by those who have less power and prestige than you have. More specifically, how are you judged by those who are under your control? When Jesus tells us in Matthew 25 that we will be affirmed or condemned on that Final Day by those who are the "least," is He not telling us that we ought to be careful about how we treat those who stand beneath us on the corporate ladder? Is He not even suggesting that, in the end, we will be judged by those over whom we "ruled"?

> There are last which shall be first, and there are first which shall be last.
>
> Luke 13:30

As a child, I loved that make-believe story of the boy prince who, through mistakes and strange circumstances, ended up having to live for a few weeks as a peasant. In his role as a poor boy, he found out the real character of those in his court. Many of those who treated him well when they saw him as the heir to the throne, treated him with rudeness and contempt when he was presented as a street waif. But he also discovered those in his court who were really good people—those who treated him royally even when he seemed to be a powerless child in rags.

Indeed, the level of our fairness is seen in how we treat those who apparently can do nothing for us or give anything to us. Fairness is when we give respect and justice to those who can provide little, if any, positive payoff for us.

Part 3

Love at Work

11

Watch Your Step

WHEN HELEN KELLER WAS ASKED IF THERE were anything worse than being blind, she answered, "Yes! Being able to see and having no vision." The Bible makes a big thing out of visions. It tells us that without them we are all dead (Prov. 29:18). Evidence of that is all too clear. Very few people these days seem to take the time and make the effort to close their eyes and visualize where they would like to go in life and what they want to achieve.

It is this lack of vision that is responsible for the diminished energy in people. Lethargy has become an epidemic. Listlessness is a pervasive condition. Everywhere we go, we encounter people who ought to change the familiar bedtime prayer of children from "If I should die before I wake," to "If I should wake before I die."

Recently, while interacting with a group of university students, I found myself growing increasingly frustrated as they talked about their lack of enthusiasm for life. They seemed bored with themselves and disinterested in anyone else. Finally, in exasperation, I shouted at them, "I'm fifty-seven and you're twenty-one, and I am younger than you are because people are as young as their dreams and as old as their cynicism. And you've got no dreams or visions."

Visions are what energize and drive us. Dreams lift us out of the doldrums and give a quickness to our walk. With God's help, you can determine your own dreams and visions. The prophet Isaiah says:

> But they that wait upon the Lord shall renew their strength;
> they shall mount up with wings as eagles; they shall run,
> and not be weary; and they shall walk, and not faint.
> Isaiah 40:31

That is why our talk about establishing a mission statement for life is so important. A mission statement is the setting down in clear and specific words the purposes and goals of life. It is a statement of what in our own eyes will make life successful. And if it is an honest and good mission statement, it can *generate such energy that even the young will be amazed.*

Coming Up with a Mission Statement

When I was forty years old, I went through a kind of mini-identity crisis. It was the sort of thing that Gail Sheehy described so well in her book *Passages.* I had been teaching sociology on the university level for more than fifteen years, and I wasn't sure that I wanted to *be* a sociologist for the rest of my life.

At one point my craving for significance drove me into politics. I didn't have any sense of calling in life, but I knew that I wanted to make a difference. As I looked over the options available to me, I decided to seek a political career. It was a kind of spur-of-the-moment decision based on the commonly accepted premise of the time that politicians are the ones who can make the greatest impact on the world.

In 1976, I entered the race for a seat in the U.S. Congress from the Fifth District of Pennsylvania. With great enthusiasm and a lot of hard work I was able to put together an interesting, if not successful campaign. Because it was toward the end of the Vietnam War, which I strongly opposed, I was able to attract a large number of anti-war activists who identified with the things I was saying.

116

The race proved to be exhausting, but also a thrill. I won the primary but was soundly defeated in the general election.

As I look back on it all, I can honestly say that I'm glad I didn't win. If I had won, I might have been trapped into a track-for-life that would have kept me from what has given me a much fuller sense of joyful purpose.

Shortly after the campaign was over, three very close friends with whom I had been having a weekly Bible study agreed to get together with me and help me think through and pray through what my life should be about. Since it was obvious that a life in politics was not going to be my future, we thought it would be a good idea to try to figure out just what I should do and be. I will always be grateful to those friends who spent long hours with me, helping me to discern what would be my life mission.

Our discussions came to a conclusion with an all-day get-together in which we hammered out some conclusions. It proved to be one of the most important days of my life because it was the day on which I was able to clearly specify what I thought would give my life meaning and what would leave me with a sense that I had run the course when I "hang up my sneakers at the end of the game."

First of all, my friends forced me to set down on paper just what I had been doing in life up to that point that had been *fun*. I know that *fun* sounds terribly unholy, but my friends and I are convinced that God has so designed us that what He has willed for us to do with our lives creates a sense of joy. I'm sure that the deliberations of theologians and biblical scholars enable them to quickly and brilliantly discern the difference between fun and joy. But for the four of us meeting together in the back room of a restaurant in St. Davids, Pennsylvania, that difference seemed insignificant.

Upon reflection I realized that I got my greatest kicks out of talking to college students. Of all the audiences that I had been privileged to address over the years, the college audiences were, for me, the most fun. I like to "turn on" collegians to God and to excite them about doing great things with their lives.

Second, my friends helped me to zero in on the primary and most significant thing that I had accomplished through my speaking to college students. I had been able to get a significant number of them to reconsider their vocational choices. My friends helped me to realize that I felt the most right about myself when I was able to get students to consider how their lives could be invested most effectively to impact others with Christ. I got my greatest high from helping collegians get a vision of the great work that they could do to further the kingdom of God.

Craig, the friend who has always pushed me hardest to define the direction of my life, would not let it rest there. "Be more specific," he insisted. "Exactly *what* do you want these college kids to do with themselves?"

Immediately, it came to me! "I want them to become missionaries!" I blurted back. "That's what I want! I want them to become missionaries!"

But Craig didn't leave it at that. "How many of them would have to go to the mission field in order to leave you with a sense that you had done what you were supposed to do with your life?" he asked.

Once again a specific number came to mind. Those with a mystical bent will say that it was the Lord speaking to me. Others, who are more positivistic in their approach to life, would simply regard the response as some sort of subconscious psychological reaction. I, personally, have to go with the mystics. The number was two hundred.

By the end of that afternoon, I had written out my mission for life, and I believe it came from God. It reads:

> Before I hang up my sneakers at the end, I want to have motivated and helped at least two hundred college and university students to commit themselves to go out as full-time missionaries for the cause of Christ.

Once my mission statement was developed, I had to face up to the fact that I needed to consider how living out that statement would affect the rest of my life.

How would it affect my family? How much time with them would I be ready to sacrifice in order to live out this mission for my life?

Obviously, some time would have to be taken away from my wife and children. I would have to think through this conflict of interests and strike up a proper balance. I would have to determine in advance just how much time I would need to give in order to be the father and husband I should be. This was not simply a matter of determining what I *ought* to do. It was a matter of what I *wanted* to do. My family has been my major source of emotional gratification. I would be sad in the depths of my being if I failed to have the relationships with them that I needed. And relationships take time.

There were other considerations. Relatives, friends, neighbors, my students, and my colleagues all required time. It was obvious that a listing of priorities would have to be established to govern my use of limited time. I had to give careful attention constantly to ensure that my priorities were reflected in my use of time and that, in the midst of living out my obligations to others, my own mission in life did not get lost.

The Peace that Comes from Definition of Purpose

Over the years I have continued to define myself in terms of my mission rather than in terms of my job. I still teach sociology, but I do not define myself as a sociologist. Sociology is something I do. It is not who I *am.*

What I *am* is a person committed to challenging college and university students to become missionaries. Right now I think I am best able to carry out that mission by teaching sociology at a Christian college. However, if I should lose my position as a sociology teacher, I do not think I would lose my identity.

My mission is what gives me my identity, and even if I lost my job, my mission would still be there. If they closed down the college where I teach, I would still be committed to challenging young people to be missionaries. If I stopped teaching sociology, I would just have to find another way of doing it. In reality, I already have. While interacting with students in a classroom setting has provided an excellent opportunity for challenging young people to become missionaries, over the past couple of years, I have found an even more effective means of carrying out my mission. And that is through being on the speakers' circuit for youth conferences. I have even considered giving up teaching sociology and concentrating completely on being a speaker, because in many ways, I feel that in that role I am more effective in promoting the missionary challenge.

I love Eastern College, but changing jobs would be no big deal for me. My identity is defined by my mission, and my mission will remain constant regardless of what job changes I make or what roles I may be led to play.

Working out a mission requires time. Jesus took time to fully grasp His mission. That is what the forty days in the Wilderness was really all about. Even the Son of God had to spend time in private prayer and reflection before assuming His messianic role. It is important that you block off sufficient time for such a crucial task. A week of restful introspection would be ideal. But if you can't do that, at least take a weekend to do it.

Second, it is essential that you get into the right state of mind, or should I say, "a state of receptive consciousness." You must become centered on God. Other things must be set aside. After all, what you are really seeking is His will for your life. Most likely you already believe that there is some ultimate meaning to your life, and in this working out of your mission statement, you will want, more than anything else, to get some inkling as to what that meaning is.

For me, stillness is what best gets me ready to be touched by God. Being still—I mean *really* still—is for me the best spiritual exercise. Being still is more than what comes from the cessation of noise. It is something that goes on inside. It happens when I let my mind quiet down.

If I sit still with my eyes closed and just think of the name of Jesus, if I say His name over and over lovingly, if I submit to the calming feeling that seems to flow into my life as my mind becomes fixed on Him, if I emotionally surrender to a sense of His presence, then stillness overtakes me. My mind stops bouncing around like a Ping-Pong ball and, in the quietude that follows, I can sense that "soft, still voice" at the ground of my being. Then, in the context of inner peace I can hear Him listening. An inaudible whisper is felt in my soul. And I know I am in touch with Him.

I have a friend who gets tuned in to the Spirit by reading from the Book of Psalms. I suppose to be more accurate, I will have to say *praying* through the Book of Psalms. He treats each of the Psalms as a prayer that the writer wrote to express his feelings to God and to verbalize what he really wants from God. "The Psalms," he says, "enable me to ask of God His most precious gift—Himself. Through the Psalms I find the words to pray for nothing except that He be with me and in me."

I recently talked to an elderly woman who finds that in reciting the words of old hymns her mind becomes open to the voice of God. She says that when she wants to feel God's abiding nearness, all she needs to do is to repeat the stanzas of a favorite hymn.

I really cannot prescribe what will work for you. Try any of the above. Try all of them. Try none of the them and come up with your own special way. There is no formula or chant that is ordained as *the* way. Jesus said:

> The wind bloweth where it listeth, and thou hearest the sound thereof, but canst not tell whence it cometh, and whither it goeth: so is every one that is born of the Spirit.
> John 3:8

In the end, a special kind of listening will be learned. Nobody need teach you. Indeed, nobody *can* teach you. This is the work of the Holy Spirit. Trust Him. Wait patiently upon Him (Ps. 40:1). In the words of the Scripture, "In all thy ways acknowledge him, and he shall direct thy paths" (Prov. 3:6).

When each time of stillness is ended, write down what came to you. Keep a journal of these times of visitation. The seeds that are planted are easily lost. Jesus explained:

> And he spake many things unto them in parables, saying, Behold, a sower went forth to sow; And when he sowed, some seeds fell by the way side, and the fowls came and devoured them up: Some fell upon stony places, where they had not much earth: and forthwith they sprung up, because they had no deepness of earth: And when the sun was up, they were scorched; and because they had no root, they withered away. And some fell among thorns; and the thorns

sprung up, and choked them: But other fell into good ground, and brought forth fruit, some an hundredfold, some sixtyfold, some thirtyfold.

Matthew 13:3–8

Test the Spirits

I believe in *koinonia*. *Koinonia* is that special event that can happen when your spiritual kin lovingly share themselves with you, and you share yourself spiritually with them. *Koinonia* is what you can experience when God confirms what He said to you in private by repeating His truth through these partners in faith.

As I drew up my mission statement, my small *koinonia* group, and especially my friend, Craig, played a crucial role. Not only did they give me assurance that my mission was a right one and fitting for me, they also helped me work through some of the means through which that mission might become a reality in my everyday life. They helped me decide that my job at Eastern College was the right place for me in the larger context of my mission.

In this latter task they were particularly helpful. That small circle of friends who make up my support group helped me to discern the difference between a real sense of leading from God and what might be merely the inclination of my own ego.

Almost two thousand years ago, people asked a man named John who he was. His answer was, "I am a voice crying in the wilderness, Prepare ye the way of the Lord."

John was a man who had a clearly defined mission. The one to whom John pointed as he carried out his mission had an even clearer definition of what He was about. Jesus said, "The Son of Man is come to seek and to save that which was lost."

Jesus knew that His mission was to initiate the Kingdom of God. He did what He was sent to do by His father. And in the end, He could shout in triumph from the Roman cross, "It is finished."

Each of us must follow the example of our Lord. Each must set forth in clear and distinct terms the life mission that will be the basis for our own self-definition. And then, each of us must

122

commit ourselves to live out our individual mission. Each must be able to say in his or her everyday life:

> Forgetting those things which are behind, and reaching forth unto those things which are before, I press toward the mark for the prize of the high calling of God in Christ Jesus.
> Philippians 3:13–14

12

Make Your Job Fit Your Mission

ERIC FROMM, THE FRANKFURT SCHOOL PSYCHOLOGIST, made it clear in his book, *The Art of Loving,* that what happens to us emotionally during our hours on the job is, in most cases, what determines how we will relate to people during our off hours. How wives and husbands treat each other, what children feel from their parents, and even how people talk to the clerks at the supermarket are all affected by what goes on at the office or at the plant.

Of course none of this is really new to us, yet the *extent* to which what we do at work structures our personal character proves to be much greater than is usually imagined. We like to think that our disposition toward life, our values and our general personality makeup are all developed in the home, perhaps with the help of the church. Most of us try to convince ourselves that the kind of person we are is solely a matter of the will, and in one sense, that may be true. But in reality, the kind of people we become is highly influenced by what happens to us day in and day out as we play out our vocational roles. That is why choosing where we work, with whom we work, what we produce, how we produce it, and how we will be involved with those with whom we work are decisions that have far-reaching significance.

Some years ago I had a young idealistic student in class named Ralph. During his undergraduate years, he was committed to becoming an advocacy lawyer who would champion the rights of the oppressed and stand up against the exploitation of the poor. This student was full of passion for justice and radiated a compassion for the underdog that inspired all who knew him. But by the time he graduated from law school, Ralph was deeply in debt, so he took a job with a large firm that specialized in corporate law and did as little *pro bono* work as possible. The pay was mind boggling, and Ralph convinced himself that he would only stay with the firm for as long as it took him to make enough money to pay off his school bills. He assured me that the yuppie subculture into which he was jumping would not rub off on him. He was certain that who he was had been so firmly established that "they" couldn't change him one little bit.

Well, you can imagine the rest of the story. When I met Ralph a few years later he was a transformed person. His idealism was gone. He let me know that he was on the verge of becoming a partner in the firm, that he had a live-in relationship with one of his colleagues, and that they had just moved into a "super place up on the East Side." What really made me sad was that the excitement that had once seemed to sparkle in his eyes seemed gone. Maybe it was my biased imagination at work, but to me, Ralph seemed to have become one of those dull, cynical, arrogant sophisticates who deem themselves to be a notch above the rest of humanity. His job had changed him. What he did, where he did it, how he did it, and with whom he did it had converted him. Oh, Ralph still went to church regularly. He had found one of those churches that served, as they say, "a better class of people."

Of course it is also true that what goes on in the workplace can change persons for the better and even make them into godly people. An ongoing relationship with associates who are kind and considerate, doing work that contributes significantly to the well-being of others, or produces things that people really need can transform us into persons who are humane and committed to justice.

The missionary organization that I lead is strongly committed to serving underclass children and teenagers who live in the slums and government housing projects that lie in the heart of urban America. Time and time again college students come to us who want to work in our programs because the work seems adventuresome. Usually these young people understand very little about the religious values that motivate our programs and condition what we do. We usually take on these young people because we know it is only a matter of time before they will be converted.

The change process occurs without these young men and women even knowing what is happening to them. As they work alongside persons whose whole reason for living is to help others, as they themselves do things that bring fun and help to urban children who have had difficult and painful lives, and as they encounter God presenting Himself sacramentally through the poor and beaten-down people in the neighborhood, they themselves are impacted. Their personalities change.

While it is more than possible for us to change the places where we work and to help those who are at our side from nine to five, it is far more likely that *we* will be changed by where and with whom we live out our vocational lives. *You are free to choose where you work, what you do, and with whom you will work. But who and what you become is hanging in the balance. Before you take a job or position, remind yourself that what will go on in the workplace will change you, and ask yourself whether or not the change will be in harmony with your mission statement!*

When trying to figure out which job is right for you, the first thing you have to do is take stock of your gifts.

What are you equipped to do?

What comes easy?

What do you really enjoy?

As you seek answers to these questions, you ought to be able to get a pretty good handle on what you should be doing with your life.

Put simply: A job that lets you exercise your God-given talents and abilities while carrying out your personal life mission is probably a good job for you to consider. And contrariwise, there are few mistakes that you can make that will create more unhappiness for yourself and havoc for others than going ahead with a vocational choice that demands of you what you cannot do well and what you really do not enjoy. (Incidentally, these two things usually go together.)

The consequences of being forced to do what is inappropriate with respect to one's innate gifts and talents is humorously illustrated by a story that educators love to tell. It is called Animal School.

The animals got together in the forest one day and decided to start a school. There was a rabbit, a bird, a squirrel, a fish, and an eel. They formed a board of education and tried to create a curriculum.

The rabbit insisted that burrowing in the ground be in the curriculum. The fish insisted on swimming. The squirrel insisted that perpendicular tree climbing be included, and the bird wanted flying.

They put all these courses together and wrote a curriculum guide. Then they insisted that all of the animals take all of the subjects.

Although the rabbit was getting an A in burrowing, perpendicular tree climbing was a real problem for him; he kept falling over backwards. Pretty soon he became brain damaged from these falls, and he couldn't burrow well any more. He found that instead of making an A in burrowing, he was making a C. And, of course, he always made an F in perpendicular climbing.

The bird was really beautiful at flying, but when it came to burrowing in the ground, he couldn't do it so well. He kept breaking his beak and wings. Pretty soon he was making a C in flying as well as an F in burrowing. And he had a very bad time with perpendicular tree climbing.

The squirrel was terrific at perpendicular tree climbing, but was so afraid of the water that he failed swimming altogether.

The fish was easily the best in swimming class, but he wouldn't get out of the water to come to any of the other classes.

The valedictorian of the class was a mentally retarded eel who did everything in a halfway fashion. But the teachers were happy because everybody was taking all the subjects in their broad-based educational curriculum.

What more need be said about being put into a work situation wherein you are supposed to do things that you are not equipped to do?

I have some friends who are highly educated professionals. They fully expected their son to follow after them, graduate from a prestigious university, and assume a vocation in some high-status profession. But as the boy moved through his teenage years it became obvious that academics were not his thing. Instead, he loved tinkering with cars.

His parents were not about to see their son become an automobile mechanic. They talked and pressured him into going to college. After a lackluster five years in an academic program that he could not wait to end, he tried to make a living at a variety of white-collar jobs in the business world.

He never worked out well in any of his jobs. He seldom seemed happy. And the only real enjoyment he got out of life appeared to be the good time he had on weekends when he was allowed to work on his car. I think the Kingdom of God is missing a happy mechanic.

Contrast this unfulfilled businessman with a young man who came to work with me in the ministry that our missionary organization, the Evangelical Association for the Promotion of Education, sponsors in Haiti.

Sandy was a Canadian. I came to know him through his cousin, who was my secretary. He had been kicking around in various jobs, and none of them seemed to fit him.

When Craig, my associate and friend, talked with Sandy, he found out that this young man wanted nothing so much as to be in a place where he was really needed. He wanted to help people. When Craig inquired as to what Sandy enjoyed doing and what his skills might be, it seemed obvious that he was one of those jack-of-all-trades who loved to fix things and make things work.

Within a matter of weeks we had Sandy placed in Cap Haitien, Haiti as the manager of a small toy factory that we had started in order to provide jobs for poor people. Years have passed. Sandy is still there. The little factory employs a dozen men. He is helping a dozen families to live above the poverty line.

Sandy's ability to fix things is constantly in use. He keeps alive an old truck that should have died long ago. He maintains the wood-working machinery of the factory so efficiently that workers never have to miss a day's work because of a break-down. His involvement with a local church has enabled him to integrate his work with the mission of the Kingdom of God.

Sandy, quite correctly, sees himself as a unique kind of missionary who helps the church build the Kingdom of God in Haiti by creating jobs.

Help for Those Who Want It

Determining your interests and abilities need not be left to some mystical revelation by the Spirit of God. Tests are available—all kinds of tests. There are tests to measure aptitude. There are tests to measure attitudes. There are tests to tell you what jobs you would be good at and what you would enjoy doing. The career planning department of your local community college or university can either provide you with the necessary testing or tell you where you can go to get help.

Determining what you are good at doing is a necessary step if you are to live out your mission in life. It is essential that you know the gifts with which God has endowed you.

I believe that God usually calls people to do what they are equipped to do. An example of this principle is David, a young man who was headed for the Christian ministry. His father, a Baptist minister, had died when David was quite young, and his mother had laid quite a guilt trip on him that it was his duty to carry on his father's work.

David tried. He really did! He did the college and seminary work that was necessary for ordination. And for more than five years he served a small struggling church in rural Pennsylvania.

But from the very beginning of his ministry, it was obvious that preaching was not his game. David literally became sick every Sunday morning, and his preaching was so dull and pointless that his congregation was not fed very well either. After five miserable years not only was his church on the verge of collapse, but his wife was about to leave him. She found no joy in a relationship with a man who was constantly miserable.

Fortunately, the bishop who supervised this young pastor's ministry recognized the problem and urged David to go to a special counseling center designed to help men and women to evaluate their experiences in the ministry. After a battery of tests and several days of intensive counseling, the young man had some very important questions answered.

Under careful direction David was able to set down his mission for life. As he stood back from what he had been pressured to be, he was able to define his real calling as being someone who would help others to go to the mission field. David very much was attracted to the idea of being part of a support system that would enable others to carry out the Great Commission (Matt. 28:19–20) and do missionary work overseas.

David also discovered through the testing process that he was not a public person. In reality he was shown to be a very private person who enjoyed working alone. Furthermore, he discovered that he had a keen aptitude for working with numbers. The left side of his brain was exceedingly active, and his capacity for logical figuring proved close to brilliant.

It was not long before David resigned his church and went back to school to study accounting. Today he serves as the comptroller of a major missionary relief organization. He has given to this organization an analytical service that has resulted in streamlining the structures of all of its ministries. David's work has been instrumental in saving the organization hundreds of thousands of dollars, thus enabling the saved money to be used to finance additional missionaries who wanted to go to the field.

Religious Vocations in the Secular World

For those with deep religious roots, one of the most difficult issues to handle is how to live out a life of service to God while holding a job in what is usually called the secular world.

Over the years, most of us have been indoctrinated with the false idea that Christian ministry is something that those who go into church-related vocations do. We usually divide the world into the sacred and the secular, and then expect the people who want to serve God rather than mammon to take jobs in the former sector rather than the latter.

Of course, this division is completely artificial so far as any careful reading of the Bible is concerned. The Scriptures teach that Jesus Christ is Lord of all, not just the Lord of things religious. When the Bible teaches us about the kingdom of God, it declares that those who would be followers of Christ are to invade all sectors of society and function as agents of change. The task of the disciples of Christ is to be His instruments for transforming society through their presence in it. That is what lies behind Jesus' teachings in the Sermon on the Mount when He says:

> Ye are the salt of the earth: but if the salt have lost his savour, wherewith shall it be salted? it is thenceforth good for nothing, but to be cast out, and to be trodden under foot of men.
>
> Matthew 5:13

> The kingdom of heaven is like unto leaven, which a woman took, and hid in three measures of meal, till the whole was leavened.
>
> Matthew 13:33

The call for those who follow Christ is to permeate society with new values and to try to restructure institutions in accord with the principles established in the Scriptures. That means that teachers will work to change the school system and make it a place where every pupil is valued and encouraged to fulfill his or her potential in a milieu that is, both personally and academically, as rewarding as each teacher can make it.

It means that business owners will put things like justice and fairness above profits and will operate within a system that communicates the message of justice for all. Such a business world will embody in its structures the kind of employment practices that reflect the principles of equality for all persons regardless of their religious, ethnic, or class identities.

It means that there will be doctors and lawyers who are committed to transforming their professions so that the services they render are just as available to the poor as they are to the rich.

It means that those in labor unions will endeavor to get their unions to abandon postures of anger and meanness toward management and will, instead, try to be agents of reconciliation. Good union members will champion the rights of other workers, but they will always do so in the context of fairness.

The examples could go on and on. Suffice it to say that the real work of transforming the world into the Kingdom of God is the work of the laity rather than the work of the clergy. In Ephesians 4:11–12 we read:

> And he gave some, apostles; and some, prophets; and some, evangelists; and some, pastors and teachers; for the perfecting of the saints, for the work of the ministry, for the edifying of the body of Christ.

What these verses tell us is that church vocations are not the primary vocations for Christian service. Those with the gifts of preaching, prophecy, and teaching, as well as the other gifts, have been endowed so that they can *build up the saints* for the work of the ministry.

The saints are the laity. They are those seemingly ordinary people who have taken their vocational place in what has wrongly been labeled the secular world. The saints are the people who, according to this passage, are the *real* ministers of the gospel.

Those who make their living in church vocations have to be made aware that most of the soldiers in the battle against demonic forces in this world come from the ranks of the laity. Lay people, the saints, are the ones on the front line in the task of changing society into the Kingdom of God.

Even if you want to shy away from the mandate to transform society and emphasize traditional evangelism, you still have to look to the laity as the primary agents for getting the job done. They are the ones who meet and interact with secular people on a regular basis. They are the ones who are welcomed into the workplaces where the unconverted can be met and engaged in *real* talk. And wherever and whenever there has been a genuine spiritual revival, it has been the work of the *real* ministers—the laity—that has been instrumental.

All of this is to encourage those who have chosen to define their personal mission as a major commitment to live out the gospel in sacrificial service, but who have no calling or inclination to get involved in church vocations. I have gone on this rip for the express purpose of declaring that to be "on a mission for God," as the Blues Brothers would say, does not mean that the so-called secular vocations are beyond the vale of consideration.

Consider the Options

When choosing a job that will enable you to live out your personal mission statement, you have to make your choice from available options. I have regular encounters with persons who not only have defined their mission, but have, unfortunately, concluded that there is only one job, or vocational option, that will enable them to live out their mission.

The strangest example of what I am trying to describe here is the case of a Ph.D. candidate I met who "knew" that the Lord had called him to teach Akkadian. Just in case you did not know, Akkadian is an ancient Babylonian language that has not been spoken for about three thousand years.

He told me in no uncertain terms that he felt that his mission in life was to prepare ministers of the gospel to understand and preach the Old Testament. He also let me know that if they did not know the Babylonian culture and, by connection the Akkadian language, they would not understand the context against which the Hebrew Bible was written.

When he went on to tell me that he had not yet found a job to teach Akkadian, I had to admit that I was not surprised. With tongue in cheek, I said, "You know, young people just aren't as interested in Akkadian as they used to be." There is no doubt that his employment options were somewhere between slim and nonexistent.

What Are the Costs

Jesus wanted people to count the cost before they made decisions. He said:

> For which of you, intending to build a tower, sitteth not down first, and counteth the cost, whether he have sufficient to finish it? Lest haply, after he hath laid the foundation, and is not able to finish it, all that behold it begin to mock him.
>
> Luke 14:28–29

This is very sound advice. When it comes to living out your mission in a specific job situation, it is extremely important that you do your best to try to figure out whether or not you are up to paying the price that will have to be paid.

Your family must be given special considerations. How will any job change impact the life of your partner and the lives of your children? Does your marital partner understand and identify with your personal mission statement? If taking a different job requires that you move to a new community, how will that move affect your children? Do you have the right to force others in your family to accept undesirable changes in their lives just so that you can live out your own vision of a mission in life? These are tough questions. But anyone who has gone through some watershed times and tried to establish a new direction for his or her life will understand how painfully real these questions are, and how difficult it may be to try to answer them.

It is interesting to note that neither Jesus nor the apostle Paul were married. Undoubtedly, this was because balancing off family responsibilities against what their personal missions in life were all about would have proven to be impossible. Jesus said as much to His mother when He was just twelve years old (Luke 2:41ff.). When she pressed Him to give His family special attention, Jesus reminded her that His mission would carry Him way beyond family commitments.

The apostle Paul was not married when he played out his role as primary missionary and theologian for the early church. However, we have some pretty solid evidence that Paul was once married. For instance, he was a member of the ruling religious body of Israel, the Sanhedrin. And we know that a man could not be admitted to membership in the Sanhedrin unless he were married.

Maybe Paul's wife died. Or perhaps, as some scholars speculate, she left him when he adopted the life of a radical follower of Christ. Whatever may be the case, Paul wrote to the Christians at Corinth that they should consider *not* getting married. His reasoning was that the intensity of the commitment required for the kind of discipleship to which he was calling them would lead to the neglect of wife and family.

> But I would have you without carefulness. He that is unmarried careth for the things that belong to the Lord, how he may please the Lord: But he that is married careth for the things that are of the world, how he may please his wife. There is a difference also between a wife and a virgin. The unmarried woman careth for the things of the Lord, that she may be holy both in body and spirit: but she that is married careth for the things of the world, how she may please her husband.
>
> 1 Corinthians 7:32–34

What I see happening in today's business world is that people are sacrificing their families for a whole lot less than the heavenly cause to which Paul gave the totality of his life.

I know lawyers who are so intent upon becoming partners in their firms that they put their families on hold until partnership is achieved. Sadly, too many of them discover far too late that there is not much family left when they finally get back to it.

I have seen insurance salesmen working six and seven nights a week in order to make things good for their families only to find later that their families have been destroyed in the process.

For ten years, I served as a pastor of churches. In that role, I stood by the bedside of a number of people as they faced the awesome specter of their own deaths. In those last moments, I have heard people say all kinds of things about what they wished they had been and done. But never once did I hear a salesman say, "Oh, if only I had made a few more calls and racked up a few more sales." Never once did I hear a lawyer wish that he or she had taken on a few more cases or written a few more briefs. Never once did I ever come across a businessperson whose deepest regret was that he or she did not open up a few new branches of the business or carry an additional line of stock.

When people are dying, they usually wish that they had done more for their families. In my experience, that is *always* what they talk about. They regret that they didn't give their children enough time when they were growing up. They talk about how they took their wives and husbands for granted and did not give them adequate affection and attention.

As you develop a statement of your personal mission in life and consider what jobs you might take in order to carry out that mission, have you figured out the costs to your family and have you asked the question, "Is it worth it?"

Obviously, being a member of a family requires individual sacrifices. You will have to make some sacrifices so that other members of the family can live out their missions in life, and each of them will have to make some sacrifices for your sake. The important thing is that you consider whether or not what you are doing with your life is worth what they have to sacrifice.

When you made up your mission statement did you forget your family? In the end, is not your family really a vital part of what your mission in life is all about?

How will your church life be affected by the requirements of your job? I, for one, think that you should give special attention to this cost factor. Church can be an essential part of your life. Your participation may well be crucial in helping you to develop those character traits that will make you the person you want to be. Your church can be decisive in molding the way your family will live and the kind of values your children will espouse.

Earlier I mentioned how the church my family attended during my childhood celebrated communion monthly and linked that observation with a congregational reading of the Church Covenant. One phrase of that covenant still rings in my mind. It concerns our commitment to that rather ordinary group of people from our neighborhood whom we called brothers and sisters in Christ. It reads, "I will give the church priority over all other institutions of human origin." That is a powerful statement and it is part of who I am.

Will a new job force you to leave a church where you belong? Will it require that your children lose friends in the church youth group who have been instrumental in influencing them for good? Will it mean that your marital partner must disengage from those people at church who are essential for his or her spiritual well-being? And will it mean that you yourself become religiously disconnected?

Even if you do not move to a new place, you have to be realistic about the extent of your time commitments. Some jobs leave no time for church activities. Some do not even allow for regular Sunday morning worship. Have you really weighed the consequences of such realities? Remember that Jesus has a question for you: "What doth it profit a man if he gain the whole world and lose his own soul?" Are the effects on your church life so great and so negative that you must conclude that the new position just is not worth it?

In your personal mission statement, was there room for the church? Was there a commitment to reaching people in your community with the love of God? Was there any decision made regarding service to others? Remember, all of these things take time, and in the end, you have to consider whether or not your job leaves room for such necessary commitments.

What About Your Friends?

Next, there is the consideration of friends. When you take a job, does it allow for the maintaining of relationships with those dear and special friends upon whom you depend even more than you depend on some of your relatives?

Jesus certainly considered friendship a very important priority. When He wanted to honor His disciples with the highest title He could assign to them, He gave them the title "friends" (John 15:15).

In the end, Jesus placed friends above all other relationships—even marriage. He tells us that marriage will not exist in heaven (Luke 20:34–36), but we know that friendship will. Which, incidentally, means that if your marriage is to have ultimate significance, you had better make a friend of your mate.

In the lives of Christians, friends are often most decisive when it comes to the strength and support that is necessary to remain faithful to the will of God. If we are to live out our personal mission statement, the counsel of friends is crucial, because friends are the ones who will hold us accountable to live consistently with that statement and will correct us when we go astray.

Friends are at the core of our lives because they love us even after they really know us. Friends are those people whom we can always depend upon to *be there* when we need someone to be there.

A man from Chicago wrote and told me about a friend that he had when he was young. He and his friend grew up as inseparable buddies from childhood through high school. And when World War I broke out, they joined the army together. They were assigned to the same fighting unit and together went to the front to face the enemy. He wrote:

> One night while on patrol, our unit was ambushed. Shots rang out from all directions. Fortunately, most of us fell into the ditch that served as a trench and provided us with protection from the bullets that whizzed overhead.
>
> Then, out in the darkness, I could hear my friend, Jim, calling for help. He kept on calling my name. He kept on crying, "Gerry! Come and help me! Gerry! I'm dying! Help!"
>
> My captain ordered me to remain put. He told me that there was no way I could save Jim and I would only get myself killed.
>
> But Jim kept calling me and I kept begging my captain to let me go. Finally, in exasperation, he gave up and said, "Okay! If you want to get yourself killed, go ahead."
>
> I crawled across the ground in the darkness, got Jim and dragged him back to the ditch. After pushing him to safety, I fell into the ditch on top of him. It was then that I realized that Jim was dead.

The captain yelled at me. "See! I told you there was no point to going out there. You risked your life. And for what! He died anyway."

But I told my captain that I had done the right thing. "When I got to Jim," I told the captain, "he was still alive. And the last thing he said to me was, '*Gerry, I knew you'd come.*'"

You can count on friends. They are hard to come by. They take time to nurture. They should be treated with loving care.

If you move, you will find it easy to make new acquaintances, but it is far more difficult—sometimes even impossible—to find new friends.

When you take a new job, how will it influence your relationships with friends? Will the new job mean an end to some friendships? Oh, I know that we all say that friends will always be friends. But if you assume that, you are making a mistake. Friends will be there if you are there for them. Will your new job let that happen?

Then There Is Money

Consider how your new job will change your life so far as income is concerned? There are those individuals who believe that money does not matter and that, if their new jobs help them to better live out their personal mission statement, then money is not worth even talking about. However, it is a serious mistake not to give consideration to finances. "Money isn't everything," as they say, but it does, among other things, keep you in touch with your kids. And if those kids are still living at home with you, you'll need more money than you might have imagined.

You should know that arguing over money is the most often cited cause for divorce. Married persons seem to have more difficulty agreeing on matters of how money should be spent than in any other area of their lives together.

Money affects the freedom that you have. It is both freeing and enslaving. On the one hand, money can deliver you from some boring, everyday jobs, like cleaning the house or cutting the grass. But on the other hand, money can get you piles of things that need major amounts of time for maintenance. Two cars require a lot of work to maintain. Taking care of a big house requires a large amount of time. Tending stocks, bonds, and real estate holdings all claim huge numbers of hours.

It is no wonder that Jesus taught us that many have their spiritual life choked out of them by "the cares of this world" (Matt. 13:22). His confrontation with the rich made Him aware of just how controlling our fiscal assets could be.

> Children, how hard it is for them that trust in riches to enter into the kingdom of God! It is easier for a camel to go through the eye of a needle, than for a rich man to enter into the kingdom of God.
>
> Mark 10:24–25

What we have to understand is that there are a lot of good things that money *can* buy, and conversely, there are a lot of good things that money *cannot* buy. If we keep our perspective on money, we will be all right:

Money can buy a house—it cannot buy a home.

Money can buy a clock—it cannot buy more time at the end of life.

Money can buy you companions—it cannot buy you friends.

But money *is* important. And before you take a new job, you have to ask if it will allow you to afford the kind of life that you honestly believe will be good for you and for your family.

On the other hand, perhaps it *would* be better to cut your income significantly and have more time for those in your life who really matter. Maybe you could get along with a lot less money and be more able to give your family what they really need in life—you!

It is hard to strike a balance so that you have enough. You should not allow your family to suffer because *you* are determined to live out *your* dream and follow *your* vision. But neither should you sacrifice what will make you a whole person in order to get enough to buy extra things that your kids might be better off without. It is a difficult thing to be willing to make *personal* sacrifices and, at the same time, to guard against sacrificing the well-being of those you love and who depend upon you.

Living out your mission will require a lot of tough decisions. One of the hardest is, "What job should I take?"

Remember something once said by a very wise man:

He is no fool who gives up what he cannot keep to gain what he cannot lose.

13

When You Get Where You're Going, Have You Arrived?

ONE OF THE STORIES I LOVE MOST IS ABOUT a missionary who came home to England after years of faithful service in Africa. Aboard the same ship on which he sailed home was none other than Teddy Roosevelt, returning from one of his famous safaris into the Dark Continent.

As the passengers disembarked in Southampton, there was a crowd of admirers waiting to greet the American celebrity. A band was playing. Confetti and streamers were thrown into the air. The cheers of the crowd were deafening. But when it was time for the missionary to step ashore, there was not a single soul there to meet him. The welcoming committee of the missionary society that had sent him to Africa had become confused about the date on which he was to return to England, and, therefore, were not on hand for his arrival.

The parade with the band playing and people carrying Teddy Roosevelt on their shoulders marched off, leaving behind a very lonely missionary. He sat on his trunk for several hours, and when nightfall came he realized that he would have to make his own way to London. Discouraged, he buried his head in his hands and moaned, "God! I didn't expect a band or a parade. But you could have seen to it that *somebody* came to welcome me home!"

Then, said the missionary, I heard God say to me, "My child, *you're not home* yet!"

I am a firm believer that the ultimate rewards for what we do lie beyond the world we know. I believe in an eternal time and place where our works do follow us (Rev. 14:13). Whatever we do, we must keep in mind that there is a future beyond this life that establishes ultimate judgment on what we have said and done. When I was a boy, my mother often sang an old gospel chorus to me:

> With eternity's values in view, Lord,
> With eternity's values in view.
> May I live each life for others,
> With eternity's values in view.

Judging Ourselves at the End of Life

There is another judgment to be considered. It is by no means even close to the importance of the ultimate judgment of God that we all have to face. But it *is* important, nevertheless. This is the judgment of our lives that we ourselves will make in the face of death. And this self-judgment haunts us more than we care to admit.

Most of us do not want to think about dying. In many ways, we work extra hard to try to keep the awareness of the eventual end of our earthly life from our consciousness. Our mortality is an incredibly heavy fact of life that we would just as soon pretend does not exist. That is one of the reasons we keep so busy and work so hard. We are afraid that if we ever stop our incessant round of activities, the fear of death will come crashing in on us. Sören Kierkegaard once said:

> We are all like smooth pebbles thrown across the surface of a pond. We skip and dance along the surface until we run out of momentum. Then we sink to a hundred thousand fathoms of nothingness.

Or, as Helmut Thielicke wrote:

When You Get Where You're Going, Have You Arrived?

> We all make noise on New Year's Eve. We are trying to drown out the macabre sounds of grass growing over our graves.

This is all on the down side of facing death. It is about the *angst* that the existential psychologists say lies at the base of most of our phobias and depressions. But there is another side to death. There is a creative and helpful way to look at what will happen at the end of life.

If we would stop and *imagine* our own dying in advance, reflecting upon what we will deem to be important to us then, we could learn a great deal about what should be important to us now. If we could posture ourselves at the end of life right now and, in our imaginations, reflect back on things, we would undoubtedly make some judgments that it would be best for us to make here in the present.

As strange as it sounds, we must learn to look on the positive side of dying. We need to consider how it is only by facing the oncoming reality of death that we can take stock of our lives and ask the most important questions we will ever ask about ourselves.

Those people who have talked to me about life when they themselves were near death have always told me that they wished that they had gained the perspective on life which is created by being near death much earlier. They claim that, if this had occurred, their lives would have been very different. It was better when we used hourglasses to keep the time. Clocks, with their revolving hands, create the illusion that time goes on forever. Hourglasses remind us that time is running out—and that there are important *questions that should be answered before it is too late.*

Let me tell you about one young man who was able to gain the blessings of facing death. Mel was a promising young writer in his early twenties, but he was dying of lymphatic cancer. It was estimated that he had six months to live.

Mel was a veteran who had already been dispirited by the climate of death he had experienced in Vietnam and was deeply depressed by cancer's invasion of his body. He went to New York in hopes of a medical cure, but his doctors offered him no hope.

Mel heard of a course at Union Theological Seminary for those who would be working among the dying. He went to the seminary to register for it. While there, he discovered that another course on the seemingly esoteric subject of John's Book of Revelation was being offered. It was to be taught by the very controversial Daniel Berrigan. As self-pitying as Mel was at the time, there was still in him some of the curiosity that had led him to Vietnam.

Mel arrived at the appointed classroom for the Berrigan lecture and sat with the other students. Then Dan Berrigan arrived. The hour for the class to start came and went but Berrigan said nothing. The room became strangely silent and still. Mel did not realize that it was one of Berrigan's customs to begin his classes with brief periods of meditative silence. The silence made Mel terribly uneasy.

When Berrigan's eyes settled on Mel, the young man became still more nervous. He thought perhaps the class was silent because they were waiting for this uninvited guest to leave. But Mel held his seat. When you are going to die, it can be rather freeing; you do not have to be so polite.

At last the silence was broken. Berrigan spoke directly to Mel with the simplest of questions: "What's the matter?"

Mel, who was then a very pale and woeful figure, considered a variety of responses, including, "It's none of your business." But those responses seemed both useless and truthless. So he said to this rather rude professor, "I'm dying. I'm dying of cancer."

There was no hesitation in Berrigan's response. Nor was there any sudden convulsion of sorrow or pity in his face as he said, "That must be very exciting!"

Confrontation with death, with the awful power of death present in a young life, normally brings shock and horror. People piously promise to pray. Some swallow in silence. Most flee. Few can imagine thinking, much less saying, "That must be very exciting."

For Mel, this brief impossible sentence fell into his life like a stroke of lightening. "Yes! How true! It is the most extraordinary event of my life! I have never faced death before. I have never had to answer the questions death raises." As it happened, Mel was not, in fact, so quick about getting to the cemetery. The cancer evaporated from his body nearly as fast as it had first appeared. And Mel was left with all of the insights that come from dying to apply to the rest of his life.

Consider with me, now, some of the questions that Berrigan's unexpected reply led Mel to explore—questions not often raised except by those near the end of life.

First of all, what will be your legacy? What mark will you leave on others? How will people remember you? And will they remember you the way in which you want to be remembered?

There are people who want to leave behind a monument. One may say, "Perhaps a library at some college will bear my name." Another seeks to have accomplished something so significant that history books will remind others of his or her outstanding contributions. And still another hopes to have a statue or a portrait of themselves prominently displayed where passersby can take note of them after they are gone.

All of these honors have their place, but there is something that is of even greater significance so far as what you have done in this world is concerned. And that is what those you leave behind will say about you after you are gone. Will they speak well of you? Will they remember you with affection? Will they talk of the good in their lives that is there because of you? And will they miss you? If these questions do not seem important to you now, let me assure you that they will when your life is coming to an end. Even at fifty-seven, I feel the growing significance of such questions, and I hope it is not too late for me to assure the best possible answers to them.

In the Book of Acts, we read about a man whose legacy is most desirable. His name is Barnabas. And those who knew him had this to say on his behalf:

> For he was a good man, and full of the Holy Ghost and of faith: and much people was added unto the Lord.
> Acts 11:24

We meet Barnabas three times in the Bible. The first time is when the people in the early church were facing a deep

151

financial crisis. These early Christians were enduring great persecution at the hands of their Roman overlords. Many had lost their homes and lands. Others had lost their lives. Most of them were left impoverished as a result of having been faithful to their convictions. Barnabas, who was a wealthy man, sold what he had, brought it to the disciples and laid it at their feet (Acts 4:36–37). He made what he had available to be used for those who had need.

We next meet Barnabas shortly after the apostle Paul has had his Damascus Road experience. Paul had been a ferocious enemy of the church and had persecuted Christians whenever and wherever he could. Consequently, when the people of the church heard that Paul had been converted, not a small number of them were suspicious. They undoubtedly whispered among themselves that all that Paul was doing was trying to get on the inside of their little community of faith so that he could find out their names and turn them over to the Roman authorities.

It was Barnabas who was willing to take a chance on Paul. It was Barnabas who brought Paul into the fellowship of the church when other Christians would not touch him with a ten-foot pole. Barnabas was the kind of person who believed in people and gave them a chance when nobody else would (Acts 9:26–27).

And, finally, it was Barnabas who, when John Mark had failed as a missionary and had left Paul and Barnabas to return home, was willing to give John Mark another chance (Acts 15:36–39). When Paul would have nothing more to do with John Mark, it was Barnabas who forgave and forgot and took back the failed preacher and made him a partner in ministry. John Mark went on to pen what is now the Gospel of Mark in the New Testament. And we would have lost him, had it not been for Barnabas.

Wouldn't you love to have said about you what was said about Barnabas? Wouldn't you really love to leave behind people who would say of you, "He was always there when I needed help?" or "She was always willing to give other people the benefit of the doubt and give them a chance to prove themselves?" or "He was always ready to forgive people and help them get their lives back together again?" Well, if that's what you want people to say when you're gone, you ought to start working on *your life now so as to make it happen.*

14

Efficiency Is
Not Enough

IT PROBABLY WON'T BE ENOUGH FOR YOU if all they can say after you're gone is that you were effective and ran an efficient office. It is doubtful that an office left in order will seem to be an adequate legacy for your life. Efficiency experts who get things working well do have their place, but we all know that a manager can be efficient without having a soul. A boss can make things happen but at the same time, lose sight of what is ultimate about relationships in the workplace. Consider the humorous tale of an efficiency expert critiquing a performance of Franz Schubert's "Unfinished Symphony":

> For considerable periods the four oboe players had nothing to do. Therefore, the number of oboe players should be reduced and their work spread over the whole orchestra, thus eliminating peaks of activity.
>
> All twelve violins were playing identical notes. This seemed like unnecessary duplication. The staff of this section should be drastically cut. If a large volume of violin sound is really required, this could be obtained through an electronic amplifier.
>
> Much effort was absorbed in the playing of demisemiquavers. This seems an excessive refinement, and it is recommended that all notes should be rounded up to

the nearest semiquaver. If this were done, it should be possible to use trainees and lower grade operators.

No useful purpose is served by repeating with horns the passage that has already been played by the strings. If all such redundant passages were eliminated, the concert could be reduced from two hours to twenty minutes.

If Schubert had attended to these simple matters, he would probably have been able to finish his symphony long before his death.

Do not get me wrong. Efficiency *is* important. More specifically, it is important that you be remembered as a good worker. To have done what you should have done and to have done it well is something that should be high on your list of priorities.

A Shoemaker's Worship

There was a picture that hung on the wall of my Sunday school room when I was a boy. That picture is imprinted indelibly on my memory. It was a picture of an old shoemaker with his head bowed in prayer as he sat at his workbench. There was a beam of light shining down on him which, obviously, represented the presence of God. But what made the picture truly unusual was that, moving up toward God through that beam of light, was a stream of shoes. They were ascending upward to God.

What the picture was trying to say was that the well-made shoes that the man had crafted were a sacred gift to God. What he had made at his workbench was a prayer of gratitude to the Lord. In the picture the quality of the man's work and the effectiveness of his labor were given ultimate meaning. This was a man who would be remembered for his diligent labor and the care with which he did his work. Those who wore his shoes would say good things about the way he had played out his role in the workplace.

As important, and even sacred, as your work might be, viewed in retrospect from the end of your life, it probably will not seem all that significant. Instead, it is likely that at that time you will want the people you have worked with to remember you as someone who brought into the office a special presence of goodness and kindness. You will want to be missed, not so much because you regularly greased the organizational machinery of the company, but because you made the people around you feel cared for and even loved.

Rita Snowden, the English author, describes a visit she made to a village not far from Dover. She tells how, as she sat drinking tea at a sidewalk cafe in the afternoon sun of a balmy spring day, she suddenly became aware of a most pleasant smell. It was as though she suddenly was surrounded by flowers.

When she asked where the wonderful odor was coming from, she was told that it was from the people who worked in the perfume factory. Almost all of the village citizens worked in a perfume factory in the middle of town and, at 4:30 when the workday was over, they carried the odor of the perfume with them out onto the streets.

My wish for you is that you give off such an aroma of graciousness and sensitive caring that, wherever you go, people will sense it. And, when you are gone, they will talk about how much they miss it.

Duty Is Not Enough

Another good thing that people might say about you at the end of your life is that you always did your duty. You always did what was expected of you in every assignment that you were given—and then some. Such an accolade would truly bring honor to your name.

There is a story about a Coast Guard training station in Cape May, New Jersey and what happened there the night of Hurricane Hazel. A distress message had come in from a ship that was breaking up just twenty miles off the Jersey coast. The commander of the Coast Guard station, upon receiving the message, charged into the barracks of some new recruits and shouted, "Rise up, gentlemen! Prepare to go to sea!"

A young man who had been barely initiated into the ways of the Coast Guard, responded in stark disbelief at the order.

"Sir!" he answered. "If we go out there, we may never come back!"

"Son," shouted the commander, "you don't have to come back. You have to go out!"

Duty! It's noble. And anybody who is in the personnel business knows that reliability is one of the traits most sought after in anyone being considered for a position—any position. But knowing that those we leave behind will say we were reliable is not enough for most of us. At our funerals, most of us want something much more than a good word about how well we carried out our assignments.

In my line of work I meet a number of preachers. For the most part they seem to be men of boundless energy and impressive commitment. Most of them talk about the long hours they have to put in and the relentless schedules they have to maintain in order to do all that they are supposed to do to keep their churches going and growing. But I am sadly aware that, in some cases, when their lives are over and they are being lowered into the ground, there will be children standing at the graveside who will be thinking, "He had time for everybody at church, but not for us. He did his duty to the congregation, and we just had to accept getting what was left over—and it wasn't much."

Let me share with you a letter that my son once wrote to me:

Dear Dad,

I don't know how to say this except just to come out and say it. I wish we had spent more time together when I was growing up. I don't want you to feel guilty or bad, because it wasn't all your fault. You were trying to balance your family with your career and your service for God. I was intent on my friends, my sports, occasionally my studies, and, when I got old enough, girls. Somehow we both got busy, and the time got away from us. Not always, but too often.

You worked too much. I didn't invite you to be part of what I was doing often enough. It wasn't until I dropped out of college that we realized we were down to our last chance to really be together. We made the most of that year, and to me it was the best year we ever had. That was when we got close and finally figured out who each other really was. It was great having enough time to do it.

I feel sorry for that man that you counseled who was so busy trying to save the world that he had no time for his kids. The world will always be there, but his kids won't. There really is such a thing as too late. It makes me feel even worse to know that he's sacrificing his relationships with his wife and kids in the name of Christian ministry, because I know the kind of frustration that will cause for them.

It's one thing to resent your dad's business or his hobbies or his adult friends, but how do you resent his working for Jesus without feeling bad and selfish? How do you compete with God? How can a Little League game or an afternoon walk or a few hours together baking cookies stand up against what your Dad says is his opportunity and obligation to do something important for the Kingdom? Those kids may even grow to hate God for stealing their father from them, the way they might hate another woman or alcohol, but they'll have a hard time admitting that, even to themselves, because they probably know it isn't right to hate God. Their father has probably taught them that much.

God isn't really stealing their father, of course; ambition or workaholism or a mixed-up set of priorities are, but those kids may not understand that for a long time. You are probably wondering if that's how I felt. Sometimes. But not often, Dad, because you did take me with you. You let me be a part of your life away from home. I must admit that when I see your schedule now, I'm glad you weren't such a big shot back when I was a kid.

Why do I wish we had spent more time together? You managed well enough to keep me from resenting your career. You entertained at my birthday parties. You came to my games. You and Mom created rituals that gave me a sense of security and belonging. Why do I think you should have been around more if I didn't miss you back then? It's simple, Dad. Because I miss you now.

I'm twenty-six years old. I have a wife, a career, and a life of my own. My childhood is gone now, and I can't do a thing about it. A few years ago they tore down my elementary school to put up an office building. The other night, I ran into Robin Roach, who was the first girl I ever kissed, back when we were in seventh grade, and I felt so old when she told me she was a senior analyst for a major corpora-

161

tion. There's a parking lot now in the field where my friends and I used to camp out. I'm losing my hair. Everything that was a part of my childhood is slipping away into time, and all that is left of it for me to hold onto is a bunch of old photographs and my memories.

Who I am is all caught up with those special things that happened when I was a kid, and I think about them a lot these days. It wasn't very hard for me to come up with the stories in these letters, Dad. They are the stories I tell all the time when I'm trying to explain who I am or what I think or how I feel about something.

Some of the stories are sad, and some of the memories are painful, but most of them are a joy to recall. Over the years, though, all of those images of growing up have sorted themselves out inside me, according to their relative importance. A million hours of television are forgotten, but the twenty minutes I watched the great Karl Wallenda walk the tightrope over Veteran's Stadium are as fresh in my mind now as if they were yesterday and not fifteen years ago. I spent a lot of my childhood with my buddy, John Baxter, and we can sit for hours and talk about every model airplane and every argument we ever had. Not much about school, mind you, just the things that mattered to us as boys. I played in a lot of soccer games, but the state championship game is the only one that I still know by heart, the only one that means something to me even now. I cherish that game like a treasure because, even in defeat, my team and I played with all our hearts and we were proud. I dream sometimes about blocking the shot that beat us, but it doesn't bother me anymore that we lost. It was enough to have had the experience.

The times that I remember best, though, are the times I spent with you. I love those memories best of all, Dad, and they're a big part of who I am. That's the whole point of these letters for me. My childhood is gone, and I will never be able to be with you the way I was with you as a little boy. I will never be that small, and you will never seem that big again. But I have my stories, and they comfort me when I am overwhelmed by the world, when I am too old all of a sudden, when I lose my sense of wonder. They are all I have of my boyhood, and the reason I wish we had spent more time together is that I wish I had more of them now. It isn't that you didn't do enough, you see, for I would always want more. You were the king of the world back then, the imp of fun, the man with all the answers, the one who could always fix what was broken. You made life seem magical to me.

When you die, Dad, I will surely go to pieces for a while, because I still count on you more than anyone knows, but in the end I will be all right. I will have my stories, and in them I will always have part of you, the part that tells me who I am and where I came from. I only wish there was more because what there is means all the world to me.

Love,

Bart

That ought to help put things in perspective. That ought to help you figure out what I did not sufficiently understand as my son was growing up.

Jesus once told a story of two sons. One was wayward and the other one always did his duty.

A certain man had two sons: And the younger of them said to his father, Father, give me the portion of goods that falleth to me. And he divided unto them his living. And not many days after the younger son gathered all together, and took his journey into a far country, and there wasted his substance with riotous living. And when he had spent all, there arose a mighty famine in that land; and he began to be in want. And he went and joined himself to a citizen of that country; and he sent him into his fields to feed swine. And he would fain have filled his belly with the husks that the swine did eat: and no man gave unto him. And when he came to himself, he said, How many hired servants of my father's have bread enough and to spare, and I perish with hunger! I will arise and go to my father, and will say unto him, Father, I have sinned against heaven, and before thee, And am no more worthy to be called thy son: make me as one of thy hired servants. And he arose, and came to his father. But when he was yet a great way off, his father saw him, and had compassion, and ran, and fell on his neck, and kissed him. And the son said unto him, Father, I have sinned against heaven, and in thy sight, and am no more worthy to be called thy son. But the father said to his servants, Bring forth the best robe, and put it on him; and put a ring on his hand, and shoes on his feet: And bring hither the fatted calf, and kill it; and let us eat, and be merry: For this my son was dead, and is alive again: he was lost, and is found. And they began to be merry. Now his elder son was in the field: and as he came and drew nigh to the house, he heard music and dancing. And he called one of the servants, and asked what these things meant. And he said unto him, Thy brother is come, and thy father hath killed the fatted calf, because he hath received him safe and sound. And he was angry, and would not go in: therefore came his father out, and entreated him. And he answering said to his father, Lo, these many years do I serve thee, neither transgressed I at any time thy commandment: and yet thou never gavest me a kid, that I might make merry with my friends: But as soon as this thy son was come, which hath devoured thy living with harlots, thou hast killed for him the fatted calf. And he said unto him, Son, thou art ever with me, and all that I have is thine. It was meet that we should make merry, and be glad: for this thy brother was dead, and is alive again; and was lost, and is found.

Luke 15:11–32

Please note the last few verses of this famous story. They are about the older brother—a young man who had always been reliable. But in the end, the fact that he had done his duty doesn't seem that important.

Fame Is Hardly Worth the Effort

There are so many people who make fame a goal in life. They want high visibility and good name recognition. These are people who, as suggested by one pop artist, will be disappointed if the whole world does not stand up at least once and give them a five-minute ovation. But in the end, fame is a ludicrous thing, and those whose goal in life is to achieve wide recognition and leave behind a wall covered with plaques have sold themselves far short in terms of what is really important.

Some years ago when my children were in their pre-teen years, I took them with me on a speaking engagement. When we drove into the parking lot adjoining the auditorium where, in just a few minutes, I was to hold forth, there were only three cars parked there.

"Dad!" exclaimed my son Bart, who at that point of his life was somewhat impressed with my role as a public speaker, "Nobody's come to hear you! And you're so famous!"

"Come on, Bart," responded my daughter Lisa, who has always been the realist in the family, "if Dad is so famous, where are all the people?"

"Knock it off, Lisa," Bart answered back. "It's pretty tough being famous when nobody knows who you are."

So much for fame. In the end, you will be proven to be a lot less of a big deal than you thought you were. And whatever fame you might achieve will probably be lost, and even your name forgotten, soon after you pass off the scene.

I am sure that you want something more at the end of your life than an obituary that lists your notable accomplishments and awards on page 25 of the newspaper. So let me make a suggestion. Allow me, in the next chapter, to outline at least one thing you can do with your life that will have value not only here on earth, but eternal significance as well.

This suggestion may seem strange and incredibly naive. But it is, I assure you, the one thing, in addition to taking care of your family, that can have lasting significance and which, at the end of life, you will be glad you did. Do not turn me off until I have made my case. And do not think you know exactly what I am going to say until you have heard me out.

Putting it to you directly, it is simply this: Help the poor and the hungry of the world. Please give me a chance to make the case for my claim that this is something you will be certain to value at the end of your life.

What I want to suggest is not simply for you to give away your money. If you think that will solve the problems of poor people then you haven't looked too closely at the give-away programs of both government and charities in today's world. I am going to tell you about something you can do that will be much more exciting, productive, and meaningful than even a gracious handout. So give me a chance. Read the next chapter.

15

An Incredible Secret About Life

Every great religion of the world urges its people to give to the poor. These pleas to help the poor are not so much because the poor need the help, but because we need what happens to us when we serve the poor.

A young businessman and his wife came to talk with me because they felt an emptiness in their personal lives and also because their marriage was devoid of the kind of gratifying excitement that they thought that it should have. I noticed that they had driven to our meeting in a new BMW. This couple was dressed to the hilt and between them they seemed to wear all of the symbols of financial success, from his Rolex watch to her Gucci handbag.

In the midst of our talk, I made a simple suggestion: "Why don't you sell that BMW and give the money to the poor?"

Actually, I was more specific than that. "Why don't you use the money from the sale of your car to support some children in a Third World country?"

I went on to point out that for 70¢ a day, or $20 a month, they could support a poor and deprived child in some place like Haiti or Bolivia. For just a small gift, they could feed, clothe, house, and educate some needy child and give him or her a more hopeful future. With the money that they had tied up in their luxury car, they could make an incredible difference in the lives of a really good number of kids. I tried to paint some verbal pictures of what life was like for kids in Third World countries, and the differences that their giving could make in the lives of some of them.

At first the young couple did not see the connection between their own emotional deadness and the way they had been living life. They did not see how hard it is for those whose lives are directed toward the accumulating of wealth and the purchasing of the symbols of wealth to gain any sense of lasting satisfaction. If they would become givers, I explained to them, they would find something in themselves and in their marriage which would meet their own needs.

Giving changes us down deep inside. It *is* more blessed to give than to receive. That is not just a truism stated by Jesus; it is a reality substantiated day in and day out by observing what happens to people when they give.

Erik Fromm, who by self-definition was a neo-Freudian Marxist, gave eloquent expression to this same idea in his somewhat old but still very relevant book, *The Art of Loving.* To give ourselves away in love is what enables us to overcome the sense of alienation that pervades the human consciousness. In simple language, according to Fromm, we are "wired" to be givers, and in giving we experience dimensions of aliveness that make us feel more fully human.

Fortunately, the couple who had come to see me was sold on what I was telling them. Actually, they became downright enthusiastic about it all. They sold the BMW! They designated the money for fifty poor children in the Dominican Republic and they have made an ongoing commitment to support them for years to come. In the years since our meeting, this couple has made several trips to the Dominican Republic to visit "their" children. Both of these people have been so gratified by what they have encountered in these dear boys and girls, that they are trying to figure out how they can help even more of them. They have gotten some of their business friends to do the same thing. And, yes, they are happier with themselves and with their marriage than ever before. Helping the poor has become a goal for their lives and has given them ecstatic meaning and joy.

An Incredible Secret About Life

Saint Francis and Mother Teresa in the Marketplace

Francis of Assisi discovered and expressed in the medieval era what Mother Teresa has discovered and expressed in modern times. Both came to realize that it is more of a privilege to give than it is an obligation. Both found, in responding to the needs of the desperately poor, the opportunity to experience the deepest joys and gratifications of existence. I often ask my students, "How do you think Mother Teresa gets up in the morning? Do you think she falls out of bed and says, 'Well, here goes, another lousy day on the streets of Calcutta.' Or do you think she gets out of bed full of anticipation for the good things that await her as she goes out among the poor?"

It may seem strange to recommend Saint Francis and Mother Teresa as models for people who are in business. And I can understand that you might contend that they are inspiring people but hardly examples of what you can be realistically expected to do with your life. Those who have children certainly will find it inconceivable to attempt to live lives of austere, spiritually grounded simplicity like these two saints. But I am only suggesting that you learn from them, that you discover the essence of what they are about and try to work it out in your own everyday life in the world of business. It can be done!

What Saint Francis and Mother Teresa can teach us is that the poor are sacramental. Something sacred is mediated through them to any of us who encounter them with love. As mystical as this may sound, it is readily testified to by those who have given the poor a chance to *help them.*

A friend of mine serves a church in the heart of Kansas City. The church is located in the tenderloin district of the city, and on the streets around the church there is a constant flow of street people. In response to the needs of the poor on the streets, my friend opened a soup kitchen.

The people who came to the soup kitchen soon started drifting into the Sunday morning worship service—much to the dismay of the staid members of the Old First Church.

A longstanding deacon of the church came to the pastor a little disturbed and very curious. He asked, "Why are we bringing all these people in off of the street?"

My pastor friend responded, "Because I believe that everybody deserves the right to meet Jesus and be saved."

"I know they need Jesus," answered the elderly deacon. But before he could say anything else the pastor interrupted him and said, "I don't mean them, I mean *you.*"

This little story picks up the theme of what I am trying to say. *Those who meet and serve the poor have spiritual experiences that give their lives meaning.* Jesus drives this point home with a dramatic story recorded in Matthew 25:31–46:

> When the Son of man shall come in his glory, and all the holy angels with him, then shall he sit upon the throne of his glory: And before him shall be gathered all nations: and he shall separate them one from another, as a shepherd divideth his sheep from the goats: And he shall set the sheep on his right hand, but the goats on the left. Then shall the King say unto them on his right hand, Come, ye blessed of my Father, inherit the kingdom prepared for you from the foundation of the world: For I was an hungered, and ye gave me meat: I was thirsty, and ye gave me drink: I was a stranger, and ye took me in: Naked, and ye clothed me: I was sick, and ye visited me: I was in prison, and ye came unto me. Then shall the righteous answer him, saying, Lord, when saw we thee an hungered, and fed thee? or thirsty, and gave thee drink? When saw we thee a stranger, and took thee in? or naked, and clothed thee? Or when saw we thee sick, or in prison, and came unto thee? And the King shall answer and say unto them, Verily I say unto you, Inasmuch as ye have done it unto one of the least of these my brethren, ye have done it unto me. Then shall he say also unto them on the left hand, Depart from me, ye cursed, into everlasting fire, prepared for the devil and his angels: For I was an hungered, and ye gave me no meat: I was thirsty, and ye gave me no drink: I was a stranger, and ye took me not in: naked, and ye clothed me not: sick, and in prison, and ye visited me not. Then shall they also answer him, saying, Lord, when saw we thee an hungered, or athirst, or a stranger, or naked, or sick, or in

prison, and did not minister unto thee? Then shall he answer them, saying, Verily I say unto you, Inasmuch as ye did it not to one of the least of these, ye did it not to me. And these shall go away into everlasting punishment: but the righteous into life eternal.

Ways of Helping that Make Sense for Business People

There is an ancient teaching that comes from the Hebrew tradition. It gives four ways of helping the poor.

1. The best way to help a poor person is to find that person a job. This first and best way allows the person to maintain dignity and make a contribution to others even as the benefits of having a job unfold.

2. Create a job for the poor person. This is to suggest that it is better to invent a job that might not otherwise exist than to just give a person a handout. The old Public Works Administration of the late 1930s would probably fall into this category. In the face of massive unemployment that had put hundreds of thousands of Americans below the poverty level, the government decided to act. What was done was to give these unemployed people work in public works projects. Men and women were put to work fixing roads, building bridges, repairing public buildings, and participating in a host of other projects. The system worked. And, so far as I am concerned, it was vastly superior to today's welfare system that seems to destroy the sense of personal worth of those who receive its benefits.

3. Give to the poor but never let the poor know where the gifts are coming from. Keep your identity secret. While this may diminish the dignity of the person who receives the gifts, at least it does not humiliate that person. This is why Jesus instructed his disciples in the Sermon on the Mount:

Take heed that ye do not your alms before men, to be seen of them: otherwise ye have no reward of your Father which is in heaven. Therefore when thou doest thine alms, do not sound a trumpet before thee, as the hypocrites do in the synagogues and in the streets, that they may have glory of men. Verily I say unto you, They have their reward. But when thou doest alms, let not thy left hand know what thy right hand doeth: That thine alms may be in secret: and thy Father which seeth in secret himself shall reward thee openly.

Matthew 6:1–4

4. The lowest form of charity is to help the poor when the poor are made fully aware of those whose giving has provided the help. Even this blesses the giver, but the greater blessing comes from the first way of helping the poor. It is the first of these four ways of giving that I hold up for business people to follow. If you want to receive the blessing that comes from helping the poor, find jobs for the poor. Help them to stand on their own feet and to walk with their heads up.

Businessmen and women are the ones best positioned to find jobs for poor people who need them. Studies done on securing jobs show that the people who get jobs are those who have friends on the inside. People already employed in the workplace know when jobs are available and the person to see to apply for them.

However, in these days, available jobs that pay enough to enable people to support their families are becoming few and far between. With thousands of jobs being exported to Mexico, and to Third World countries because of the low costs of labor there, viable employment opportunities may not be readily available. There are always employment opportunities for low wages and without hospitalization and medical benefits, but relatively unskilled workers have a very hard time finding work that pays enough to support a spouse and kids.

It was because of this reality that some of us at Eastern College, where I teach, initiated a master's degree program to provide the training and skills necessary for a person to become an entrepreneur among the poor. Those who are in this program are learning how to go among the urban poor here in the United States and start cottage industries and microbusinesses in their neighborhoods.

The task for which we are training our students is one that can be carried out effectively by persons with business experience. Of course, they will have to be special people. They will have to have what the old-time revivalists used to refer to as "a call."

It is a call to leave the comfort some of the posh suburbs of America offer and venture into the urban ghettos of our country. It is a call to use all the connections you have to help start small entrepreneurial programs in areas of urban blight. It is a call to do what you can to alleviate the economic problems of those who live in communities where unemployment rates sometimes run as high as 60 percent.

As an example of what can be done, two of my Eastern College students have gone into a government housing project and started a small t-shirt factory. This little factory produces customized t-shirts for organizations like churches and bowling teams and has provided employment for a half-dozen urban teenagers.

Another example can be found in Camden, New Jersey, the city that *Time* magazine called one of the worst places in America in which to live. There a young printer named Nick Purcell, who left the comforts of home in Vancouver, Canada to become an urban missionary, has started a print shop. African-American teenagers as well as a half-dozen Hispanic women have designed and produced some very elegant note cards. And the sale of this stationery is giving some poor urban folk a measure of hope for their future.

Part-Time Entrepreneurs
for Biblical Justice

While what is being done in the t-shirt factory and in the print shop is impressive, the real answer to the needs of the urban poor will not be solved by such full-time "missionary" entrepreneurs. What is needed is for those who are gainfully employed in regular businesses to use their expertise to create jobs.

Imagine four or five persons with a knowledge of bookkeeping, marketing, management, and production forming an advisory committee that would provide guidance and financial backing to start up a couple of small businesses. Let me just name a few possible options:

Rewinding burnt out alternators and generators for automobiles.

A moving business

A home or office cleaning business

Recharging cartridges for computer printers

Lawn and garden maintenance service

Car wash

With a little imagination, a small team of committed persons could dream up scores of suggested businesses that would require little financial capital. And these businesses could provide decent paying jobs in neighborhoods where people have been cut off from the American Dream.

These new businesses could easily be "housed" in urban churches. There are tens of thousands of such churches in cities all across the country that hardly use their buildings from Sunday to Sunday. Often there are numerous Sunday school rooms that were needed during the glory days of these churches, but now have little use. A given church might serve as an incubator for four or five businesses at a time. Most inner-city churches have well-equipped offices with machinery (typewriters, computers, duplicating machines, etc.) that could be used by these new businesses, thus cutting down on overhead costs.

Having researched microbusinesses for the urban poor, I know that there are ways of incorporating them so that the churches that house them are not endangered by possible liability suits, nor will they lose their tax-free status under the law. I believe that only committed volunteers from the business community of this country can save America from the urban crisis that threatens our future. The government, regardless of who gets elected, is on the verge of bankruptcy and does not have the means to pull off what has to be done for the inner-city poor.

The private sector is too oriented to the maximization of profits to get involved in this sort of thing. While there are profits to be made in such microbusinesses in the inner city, the profit margins will not be as good as those of businesses located in "better" communities.

Finally, there is the hassle of working with poor people, many of whom have never held down a steady job in their lives. Members of the underclass, as Oscar Lewis, the famous anthropologist, points out, are not the easiest people with whom to work. Not only will they have to be taught the necessary skills to do their jobs, but they will have to be "nurtured" into a lifestyle that is different from any they have ever known. What is required is caring people who can spend enough time with them to shepherd them into a socially and economically viable way of life.

Think how exciting and fulfilling such a venture could be! You would, in the end, be able to look back on it all and say to yourself, "I not only made some money in my life, I also made a positive difference."

Personal Encounters of the Highest Kind

I suppose that, in the final analysis, it is not so much what you *do* for the poor as it is that you come to *know* them. Intimacy with the poor and the powerless involves you in something that has awesome potentialities for the renewal of the heart and for the energizing of the soul. I did not simply pick the idea of helping the poor from an array of themes when I sought to show where meaning and psychological aliveness might be found. I am convinced that this is the primary way to self-fulfillment and inner peace. The prophets and the truthsayers of the world cannot all be wrong. This is *the* thing to do. Serve the poor. If not in the ways I have suggested, then find some other ways. But do it!

In an arena of society where competitively achieved success is literally worshiped, this may seem like a strange and out-of-place thing to suggest. You may be asking yourself, "Isn't this the kind of stuff that social workers and the clergy are supposed to do?"

All that I can say in response is, "Self giving to the poor is too important a thing in life to be left in the hands of professionals!" We, the ordinary people in business and industry, must realize that the joy that comes to those who minister "to the least" of our brothers and sisters is a joy that *we* desperately need. We need to know that, because of us, others who were less fortunate have been enriched to live fuller lives.

Dag Hammarskjold, the one-time secretary-general of the United Nations, once declared, "When you were born, you alone cried; all others were happy. So live that, when you die, you alone will be happy and all others will cry."

Therein lies the secret of life!

16

It's Later Than You Think

Iᴛ'ꜱ ᴛɪᴍᴇ ᴛᴏ ᴍᴀᴋᴇ ꜱᴏᴍᴇ ᴅᴇᴄɪꜱɪᴏɴꜱ. Even if you do not want to, you have to make some decisions. Jean-Paul Sartre, the French existentialist philosopher, said it well when he reminded us that "not to decide is to decide." In reality, to wait is, in most instances, to let other people or circumstances make decisions for you. For instance, if you are taking your time about trying to decide whether or not to catch the twelve o'clock train, at 12:01 you will find that your decision has been made for you. And so it is with all of life. You can try to put off deciding whether or not you are going to make some necessary changes in your life. But if you put it off, you probably will find that what you were trying to decide will be decided for you.

Who Is Going to Write Your Script?

It is a matter of great urgency for you to decide who is going to write the script for your life. Who will determine what role you play on life's stage? Who will write your lines? Who will determine whether the play is a comedy or a tragedy?

Sören Kierkegaard, the Danish philosopher and a most intriguing man, once said that there are some people who are content to go to the theater and watch a play that others have written, listen to lines that others will speak, and be caught up

181

in events that others have determined. There are others, contended Kierkegaard, who want to play a major role in the play. These people are not content to sit in the audience in a passive manner. They want to be up on the stage making things happen. They want to be active. They are so anxious to identify with a major role that they are willing to forget that the lines they utter are not their own.

And finally there are still others who will not be content unless they themselves get to write the script and direct the action on the stage. These are the people who want to determine the final outcome of their own drama and will be content with nothing less than being the authors who choose what happens in the final scene before the curtain comes down.

Kierkegaard differentiates these three types of people very well. You have to figure out which type best identifies you.

Are you passive? Are you willing to let life happen while you function as a spectator? Are you content to let the curtain fall on the final act without having participated in any significant way in what went on?

Being a spectator comes easy. Being passive is to be devoid of anxiety about choices. And if this is what you want to be, you will have a lot of company. Most people like being this way. Most people decide not to decide. And most people make a virtue out of "taking life as it comes" without complaint.

Then there are those who act, but who let others write their lines. They are involved with what is going on. They are constantly in motion. They are always saying significant things. But what they say and do has been decided for them. Are you one of them?

Are you a person whose life has been prescribed by others? Did you find yourself structured by parents? Now that you are come of age have you yielded to the dictates of the company? Are you one of those persons who spends each day doing what you are supposed to do without thinking? Your day unfolds without any decision making. You go to work the same way, you smile at the same people, you sit at the same desk, and you work through the same kind of papers.

There is nothing wrong with such a routinized life if that is what you want. If you have chosen to live this way because it fits in with your mission in life, it can be a very good way to live. However, if you have drifted into such a role without thinking and now find yourself trapped in it, you may find the routine unbearable. You may then be one of those who, in the words of Henry David Thoreau, "lead lives of quiet desperation."

Finally, there are those who demand the right to write their own script. For all the stresses, strains and sorrows that sometimes come with being in this third group of persons, it is only these who come to know the glory that goes with being human beings. These are the people who become "authentic" persons because they really choose who they will be and do not simply pretend to do so. For better or for worse, their lives are really their own and they will not let anyone else determine what they say or do.

Religious people might misunderstand my praise for this third type of person. They might accuse me of lauding some kind of humanistic ideal-type individual or est disciple who claims that a person can be the ultimate master of his or her fate.

This is not at all what I am trying to say here. All I want to communicate is that the best kind of person is one who assumes responsibility for his or her life and believes in the right of every individual to exercise decision-making power and to determine his or her destiny.

To the religious, I say that even people who trust in God have a personal decision to make. Even when it comes to being a *true* person of faith, every one of us eventually writes his or her own script. The faith of parents cannot save you. Neither can membership in some church that you joined out of family tradition or because of social class identity. God can only be known to people who personally *decide* to know Him, and God can only participate in guiding the lives of those who individualistically *choose* to make Him Lord of life and Senior Partner in all of life's ventures.

Now Is the Time to Change

Which type of person you eventually become is up to you. You can change. If you have been passive you can become active. And, if you are an actor, you can become a scriptwriter. You are quite capable of rising above the lower types and becoming a *real* human being—the choice is yours.

To make the decision to assume responsibility for what you become involves tremendous risks. It is comfortable to remain passive and let the play unfold without any effort on your part. You may not like the outcome, but you can always shrug your shoulders and claim that you really couldn't help it, that you did not have the chance to make things turn out other than the way they did. What happened was out of your hands. Those who passively let life unfold, forfeit the opportunity to determine their own destinies in return for being able to escape the burdens and responsibilities that go with decision making.

Those who are actors in roles that others have defined for them also are free. They are free from any worry over whether or not they are saying or doing the right things in life. But those who decide to be actors in the plays that others write can never have a sense of having a personal mission in life that they themselves have designed. They can never have a sense that they did something noble or heroic in life even though the crowd may applaud their performances. Unless they completely delude themselves, they will always know that who and what they are is something that, for them, was never chosen.

It is to the scriptwriters of their own lives that the laurels belong. These are the daring people who realize the cost of what they decide. They know the risks involved but, nevertheless, commit themselves to living out a mission that they participated in defining.

There Are Risks in Being a Scriptwriter

Those who would dare to leave the safety of the passive audience or abandon the roles of actors whose lives are written by others must know that there are risks involved. Primarily, there is the risk of failure. To have attempted to live out a stated mission is heroic, but failed heroes are the ready targets of those who do not dare to try. Those who stand by the sidelines and play it safe want to justify themselves. In response to such reactions, Theodore Roosevelt once wrote:

It is not the critic who counts,
Nor the person who points out
  how the strong stumble,
And where the doer of deeds
  could have done better.
The world belongs to the person
  who is in the avenue.
Whose face is marred with
  dust and sweat.
Who strives valiantly,
Who may err and fall again,
Whose place shall never be with
  those cold and timid souls
  who know neither victory nor defeat.

Again, Sören Kierkegaard has some useful illustrations about what it means to take the leap of faith and make those changes in life which will orient you toward your own life's goals. After all, he is the one who coined the phrase, "leap of faith" in the first place.

Kierkegaard describes a make-believe town where only ducks lived. It was Sunday morning in Duckville and, as was the custom, all the ducks waddled out of their houses and down the streets to the First Duckist Church. They waddled down the aisle of the church, waddled into their pews, and squatted.

Shortly afterward, the duck minister took his place in the pulpit and the church service was under way. The scripture text for the morning was taken from the duck Bible and it read:

Ducks, God has given you
  wings—you can fly.
Ducks, because you have wings
  you can fly like eagles.
Because God has given you wings
  no fences can confine you,
  no land animals can trap you.
Ducks! God has given you wings!

And all the ducks said, "Amen!" And they all waddled home.

It is not enough to *hear* the good news about what you can be. You have to act on it. It is not sufficient that you clearly define your mission, nor even that you count the cost. The time is at hand to go for it. You don't have to waddle. You can fly! But in order to do so you must act on what you have thought out and concluded.

You will never be *sure.* You have to step out on faith. And faith, says the Scriptures, "is the substance of things hoped for, the evidence of things not seen" (Heb. 11:1).

You have to ask yourself if you want your future to be like your past. You have to consider whether or not you will be satisfied in the end if you remain where you are and what you are in the present. And if the answers to both of these questions is an emphatic no, then it is time to make some bold changes.

You Are Higher Than the Animals

One of the major differences between human beings and the lower animals is that we have the capacity to be influenced by the future. Animals are not that fortunate. Animal behavior is controlled by instinct. Some of what animals do is determined by their genes, and the rest is the result of being conditioned by rewards and punishments.

Humans are different. We are able to envision a future and direct all our energies and resources toward realizing that future. We do not have to simply *react* to external stimuli; we can *act.* We can will, even against incredible odds, to become what we are not and do what we've never done before. And what we have the courage to become will determine more about who we are than anything past or present.

The Bible says that we can repent of our past and that we can be redirected in ways that will be good for us and good for those who know and love us most. God will provide us with help and comfort in all of this. He will give us guidance and insight.

But, in the end, nothing will change in your life until *you* define the future that is ultimately meant for you and *will it* to become real.

Do not let anything turn you back. Do not let discouragement delay you. Do not let ridicule slow you down.

It's Later Than You Think

If you know what you want to be—then be it.

If you know what you want to do—then do it.

And if you know what you want your legacy to be—then start to create it now.

A Request from the Author

As I have indicated in this book, my life mission has been to challenge young people to serve the underclass people who reside in urban America and Third World countries. In order to carry out this mission, I have established the Evangelical Association for the Promotion of Education, an organization that gives young women and men the opportunity to be involved in inner-city ministries.

I believe that young people become "infected" by the missionary calling through being personally involved in missionary work. And I believe that by joining in the ministries of EAPE they can have this kind of involvement.

Each year, through EAPE, more than 250 collegians and other young adults join me in a variety of urban programs for inner-city children and teenagers. These include camping, sports, tutoring, entrepreneurial projects, art, drama, music, Bible study, and numerous cultural enrichment activities.

Other EAPE programs include Cornerstone Christian Academy, an alternative school for children who live in government housing projects, and thirty-seven literacy centers in the nation of Haiti.

In all of these ministries, young people have the opportunity to try out their missionary calling and to learn how work among the poor really feels.

I need help in keeping the work of EAPE alive. If you would like to be a part of these efforts by supporting them financially, I would be most appreciative.

All gifts are tax deductible. Checks should be made out and mailed to:

EAPE
Box 7238
St. Davids, Pennsylvania 19087-7238

Information on becoming a volunteer can be obtained at the same address.